What people are saying about

The Ripple of Awakening

Ann-Marie has written an extremely
book here. Anyone who has already
stepping on to their Spiritual Path

its contents. Ann-Marie has made th_ ,_..._y easy to follow
and understand with wonderful personal, and other fellow
travellers' stories, with which newcomers can relate. The journey
can be very lonely and confusing, at times, and this book will
remind the reader that they have many Mighty Companions to
accompany and support them on their journey. This beautiful
book is one of those Companions, and I can recommend it
without reservations.

John Campbell, author of *The Secret of Intimate Relationships*,
ACIM Teacher and Speaker

I have a PhD in Genetics and am a former Neuroscientist who
was firmly steeped in the belief that 'when you're dead, you're
DEAD'. My time of 'awakening' to my Spiritual aspect arrived
when I was rocked to my core following the death of two
husbands. I wish I could have had a book like this with which
to guide me at a time when I sure felt lonely!

I was such a pragmatist and non-believer, I was left totally
confused and bewildered by some of the writings I first came
across in this field, and something like Ann-Marie's book
would have grabbed me, I know that. This book, although very
sensitively written, is also light-hearted, fun and extremely
insightful. It is written by someone who has definitely 'been
there, done that and got the T-shirt', as the saying goes. I will
definitely give this as a 'gift' to anyone coming to me for support
when beginning their Spiritual Journey, or, already on it and

needing a gentle reminder.

Dr Anne Campbell, PhD, co-author of the bestselling *Brain Sex*, *Why Men Don't Iron* and *A Mind to Crime*, all under her former name of Dr Anne Moir, PhD, ACIM Teacher and Speaker

The Ripple of Awakening

A Mighty Companion on the Spiritual Awakening Journey

Ann-Marie Marchant

Winchester, UK
Washington, USA

JOHN HUNT PUBLISHING

First published by O-Books, 2022
O-Books is an imprint of John Hunt Publishing Ltd., 3 East St., Alresford,
Hampshire SO24 9EE, UK
office@jhpbooks.com
www.johnhuntpublishing.com
www.o-books.com

For distributor details and how to order please visit the 'Ordering' section on our website.

ISBN: 978 1 80341 044 9
978 1 80341 045 6 (ebook)
Library of Congress Control Number: 2021949961

A CIP catalogue record for this book is available from the British Library.

Design: Matthew Greenfield

UK: Printed and bound by CPI Group (UK) Ltd, Croydon, CR0 4YY
Printed in North America by CPI GPS partners

We operate a distinctive and ethical publishing philosophy in
all areas of our business, from our global network of authors to
production and worldwide distribution.

The Ripple of Awakening

A Mighty Companion on the
Spiritual Awakening Journey

How to Dismantle the NHS in 10 Easy Steps (Second Edition)
Youssef El-Gingihy
The story of how your NHS was sold off and why you will have
to buy private health insurance soon. A new expanded second
edition with chapters on junior doctors' strikes and government
blueprints for US-style healthcare.
Paperback: 978-1-78904-178-1 ebook: 978-1-78904-179-8

Digesting Recipes
The Art of Culinary Notation
Susannah Worth
A recipe is an instruction, the imperative tone of the expert, but
this constraint can offer its own kind of potential. A recipe need
not be a domestic trap but might instead offer escape —
something to fantasise about or aspire to.
Paperback: 978-1-78279-860-6 ebook: 978-1-78279-859-0

Most titles are published in paperback and as an ebook.
Paperbacks are available in traditional bookshops. Both print
and ebook formats are available online.
Follow us at:
https://www.facebook.com/ZeroBooks
https://twitter.com/Zer0Books
https://www.instagram.com/zero.books

For video content, author interviews and more, please subscribe to our YouTube channel:

zer0repeater

Follow us on social media for book news, promotions and more:

Facebook: ZeroBooks

Instagram: @zero.books

X: @Zer0Books

Tik Tok: @zer0repeater

Contents

Poem – Come My Love by Ann-Marie Marchant   xii

Foreword by Rev. Sarah Cox   xiii

Chapter 1: Trusting the Voice   1

Chapter 2: What is a Spiritual Awakening   7
    The First Step
    Who, What, Where and Why...?   8
    Moving Beyond Words and Labels   9
    An Adventure of a Lifetime   11
    Redefining and Rebooting   12
    Defunking God   14
    That Three-Letter Word   19

Chapter 3: Who Are You?   24
    Ego vs Love

Chapter 4: How It All Starts   28
    The Falling   37

Chapter 5: The Unfolding Begins   39
    Falling Apart   43
    Breaking Open   46
    The Calling   50
    Coming Out of the God Closet   54

Chapter 6: Authentic Self-Expression   58
    The Young Ones   67

Chapter 7: The Times They are a Changing   69
    Supporting Yourself   74
    Self-Care   75

Managing To Stay True To Yourself 79

Chapter 8: Taking Self-Responsibility 82
    Meditation and Prayer 87

Chapter 9: The Know It All Mind 94
    The Attraction Factor in Intimate Relationships 101
    Learning When To Step Back 103
    Reaping the Rewards and Time To Move On 107

Chapter 10: Building Trust and Faith 112
    Welcome Home 116
    Leap and the Net Will Appear (I Promise) 119
    Full Circle 120

Chapter 11: Moving On and Moving Through 127
    The Gift of Forgiveness 129
    A Reason, a Season Or a Lifetime 131
    An Opportunity To Heal 135
    Seeing Beyond the Illusion 138

Chapter 12: A Guiding Light 141
    Heaven On Earth 143
    Thank You
    Poem – Slow 146

Transcript of Interviews 147
    Sarah Cox 148
    John Campbell 153
    Annie Campbell 160
    Anna Grace Taylor 164
    Gabrielle Anya Rafello 168
    Kat Byles 172

Further Support and Inspiration 176
Acknowledgments 178
Endnotes 180
About the Author 182

For Daniel and Emma
Thank you for being my greatest teachers and for showing me the true meaning of surrender and unconditional love. And to you, dear reader – thank you for saying yes!

Come My Love…

Come my love
And rest with me
Lay your burdens down
In quiet sanctuary

No need to push or force
Just pause awhile
For I will be your comfort now
Just walk back home with me

And in my love, you'll be sustained
and never need to strive again
for you are my beloved child
holy, pure and true

My love supplies your every need
And fulfils your happy dream
Just be at one with me my child
And unite with me in light

For in my grace you're ever safe
And fear will melt away
Along with past and future goals
all gone without a trace

Ann-Marie Marchant

Foreword

There is a beauty in watching someone awaken to spiritual truth. It is not always pretty, and it can be a long event. Yet within the messy, painful and sometimes desperate times, there emerges a light that shines brightly out into the world and becomes a beacon of hope for others who also wish to drop their stories and become clear in knowing who they are. Ann-Marie is one such light, and it has been an honour and a joy to watch her emerge from the confines of her egoic mind to the freedom of the Universal Mind.

I first met Ann-Marie in 2004 when she arrived at my psychic training class weary, battered and confused. I have watched her walk her path with one hundred per cent commitment and focus, and so the outcome is very beautiful. Through her determination to be healthier, to live with more joy and to clear the illusions from her mind, she has created a world and life that she never thought possible. Now she turns back to all those wanting what she has found and extends a loving hand ready to help you step forward on to the path of awakening.

She describes her journey with such honesty and humour. The highs and the lows, the clinging and the letting go we all experience as each stage of the path unfolds one slow step at a time. This is indeed a mighty companion for anyone stepping on to the path but unsure where to begin and how to cope with the various stages that evolve as we tread new ground, that can feel scary to our brain which has been hardwired to expect us to suffer. Her support is hugely valuable, giving reassurance that you are not mad, that all the strange things happening to you are a normal part of your growth, and most importantly that life will get better.

As she let go of her control and limiting beliefs, her natural intuition kicked in and it took immense bravery to trust the inner voice that she began to hear. Learning to let go of people, places and stuff is part of the path she shares with you. As you "lose your mind" and the ego starts to dissolve, instead of finding that we have also dissolved into nothing, we find we can simply step through the veil of illusions and find ourselves in an expanded world which is brighter, better and infinitely more beautiful than we could have ever envisaged.

Coming out of the spiritual closet can feel a scary prospect, especially when you feel lonely and don't have much support in your daily life. You will find that the right people present themselves in perfect timing once you begin to let go of the old world. Allow Ann-Marie to guide you through your transformation as you let go. She is indeed a friend to reassure and support you at this time of your awakening.

She explains how your body, friendships and relationships change, things in your environment become unacceptable and how to release energy to live more joyously.

She shares teachers and processes that worked for her. She interviews people already well on their path who have guided her with Universal Wisdom. She documents the struggles with her own ego, and the inner voices that try to dissuade her from her path with the unrelenting stories of "not being good enough" or "feeling unworthy". We are all more similar than we realise, and this mighty companion will help you along the way.

It has been a joy watching Ann-Marie transform her thoughts and her body. Now, stepping up to her inner calling to write about these experiences she can help you with your journey to happiness. She combines her own wisdom with teachings from ACIM, Abraham, Joe Dispenza and many others, distilled into this wise manual; a loving guide to help you find the freedom you are seeking. I know you will enjoy this book and all the beautiful teaching it has to offer. I wish you well on your path to freedom.

Rev. Sarah Cox
Founder of Zephorium

Chapter 1

Trusting the Voice

There is a place that you are to fill and no one else can fill, something you are to do, which no one else can do.
Florence Scovel-Shinn[1]

It was actually 4am on a cold and frosty morning in January 2019 when I was strongly 'prompted' to get out my notebook and pen. I had learnt to listen to the prompts over the years and the short, but direct, message I received that morning was clear. It was indeed time to share my message with the world, and start writing this book.

I have to admit it was quite a daunting prospect because I had never seen myself as a writer and historically my literary experiences at school were quite basic and certainly not of 'A star' performance! But as I came to discover, this was actually irrelevant, because when Spirit guides you, there is nothing in the world that can stop the message from coming through if we are but willing to share it.

One experience that helped me trust and embrace this process was back in 2010. I was preparing to run a meditation in the beautiful bluebell woods near where I lived and thought it would be great to read a poem about bluebells. I searched online but couldn't find anything that touched me. I received a clear message in my head, "You write it!" I was dismissive of this voice at first, because I just didn't believe that I could. But again, the voice boomed inside my head: "You can do it!" To keep the voice 'quiet', I thought, what the heck, let's give it a go, and lo and behold, the words just fell on to the paper. I must admit, I was rather moved by the poem and was impressed at how easily it all happened.

Over that period of time, nature inspired me again and again, and I couldn't help but express those feelings through the medium of poetry. For the most part, I kept them all to myself as I just didn't have the confidence to share them, but little by little as I dipped my toe further into the arena of inspired writing, I began to write a monthly newsletter which included spiritual insights and inspiration to help and support other people. This tentative writing was always well received and I really enjoyed the creative process that was developing, but I just couldn't get any momentum moving on a real book! To be fair, I never felt quite brave enough to consider myself an author and had become accustomed to the very familiar ego voice of doom and gloom, which I came to discover was not the true me, but the bogus part wishing to keep me in the darkness. It came up with some real humdingers with its well-rehearsed comments like, "You write a book, you've gotta be kidding, that's what other people do and they have something of interest to say! They will also have letters after their name, a degree in literature and a literary prowess second to none..." Etc., etc., but as you will discover, as you turn the pages of this book, I have found ways to soothe that part of me and uncover its lies and attempts to keep me in littleness, and instead I have learnt to develop and trust in the 'other voice', the one that always speaks the TRUTH, the one that inspired me way back then to write my first poem. That voice is always loving, always kind and always calling us to the light.

I have chosen to let the presence and brilliance of that loving voice now be the leader in my life, and as such, I have learned to embrace the gifts that have come to the fore as a result. That journey of connection and remembering the truth of who I really am is what this book is based on, my learning from a real-time Spiritual Awakening (SA), as I feel one can only teach from one's own experience.

My intention is for this book to be a companion for those of you who find yourselves tentatively or wholeheartedly on the path of awakening too.

My words will always be authentic and real and, at times, raw, for I know that your soul wants the truth and nothing else will do. I would suggest that you take what feels right for you and disregard the rest. Please don't feel obliged to do anything that is shared, but I would encourage you to have an open and curious mind, and set an intention to listen to your own heart and build a relationship with the radical honesty that will flow from it.

Please also know that, at the core of this book, there is the deepest love and respect for those who are on the path of awakening and who are opening up to what that means. Many more people, just like you, are being called to this holy shift of the mind and have been asking the bigger questions, and as a result there is a quickening and inevitable growth in those who are awakening.

We are waking up to the Truth of who we really are, a boundless, eternal and loving Spirit of pure light. We are being called to share this Truth and shine without apology. I believe that as we wake up and walk this path home, we can't help but share and extend the Love that we are. I like to see it as a Divine ripple, which grows stronger as each one of us commits to shining our light. As we do so, this in turn radiates out into the world to those hearts who are ready to receive it.

This ripple effect is way beyond anything I could practically change in the world through action alone. The power of the word and the opening up of technology is bringing about a massive shift in how people are gaining access to information and I am excited to know that the potential for reaching those who are ready for change will be much easier than for our generation and our forefathers.

If you are to save the world, you first accept salvation for yourself.[2]

A Course in Miracles

I understand the concepts in this book may be challenging and shake some of you up, and I say amen to that! This essentially means that a shift is taking place, one that will have a profound change on what you thought you knew and open you to a consciousness that few consistently plug in to, let alone know exists. This consciousness is a powerful awareness beyond the normal humdrum of most people's lives and when one cultivates it, as I found out first-hand, miracles unfold in a multitude of ways with far-reaching consequences.

I have interviewed others who have also walked this path of awakening and who share a mutual desire to create Heaven on Earth. I felt it important to include different insights, as it shows the diversity of how a SA unfolds. I trust their truth will spark something within you and illuminate your soul in some way to remind you that there is not one guru or one way – we are all teacher and student – we are all one.

Each of their stories was given with such generosity, along with a genuine desire to help those who are awakening and searching for truth. I will intersperse these insights and wisdom throughout the book, and the full details of each mighty companion, as well as their inspiring and insightful interviews, are listed at the end of the book. (Don't skip them, as they are full of many gems!)

My heart is so full of love and admiration for these dear souls and I send each of them my sincere and heartfelt appreciation for a) walking the path with such integrity and authenticity, and b) for sharing their heartfelt truth. Each one of these people has touched my life in some way and inspired me to write this book. They have all been a guiding light when I forgot who I was, and some have helped me face challenges that I thought were insurmountable, and mirrored back to me my own light and boundless love when I had forgotten.

It has shown me that the SA journey is totally unique just like our fingerprint, but with similar themes, stages, challenges and highlights, and I felt it important to illuminate these similarities so as to reassure and support the traveller on this profound journey.

I also want to honour you, dear reader, for turning up and holding this book in your hands. At a deeper level I believe your soul is calling you home, and I pray that you find some peace, reassurance and insight into your own true self from the pages that follow. It may be a word that touches you, a whole paragraph or chapter, but trust that behind the words, there is an energy you will feel on a deeper level that is beyond form and cannot be spoken or written about. Allow this consciousness to move through you, even if at times you don't quite understand what is happening, and please trust that there is a Divine Intelligence at work, moving you to a space of inexplicable grace and bliss.

The unfolding of your journey may not always look pretty, it certainly wasn't for me, and at times you may want to run for the hills and take cover! And at other times you may feel a total sense of utter joy and release, as you come to realise that all the trappings of your conventional life are, in fact, a total construct with no basis of truth at their core.

In either case, know that whatever you have personally experienced so far is perfect and not to be compared to my journey or anyone else's. You will discover, as I did, that there are many similarities, stages and phases that share a common theme on the SA.

If you choose to say yes to your own inner mission, you will be rewarded in ways you thought you could only dream of, because you will discover a world full of joy and love, and as a result you will never feel alone or lost again. Not a bad reward, I think you will agree.

There is support with you every single step of the way as there is 'One' who stands by your side gently waiting to hold your hand and lead you home. That hand will always be there anytime you need reassurance, so learn to trust in its presence and build a relationship with it, whilst also being prepared to stand naked and undefended as you release the old version of you.

There will be many mighty companions to meet on the journey who will support you too, and who will be there to offer you a physical hand to hold on this wild ride. Don't be too proud to take the hand or too independent to ask for help – this is a time when we need our spiritual brothers and sisters to remind us what is real when we have forgotten.

If you are ready to step up and into your boundless life and extend the ripple of love, then please feel free to take my hand, and together we can take the next step in discovering a truly mystical and miraculous journey of unimaginable depth and vastness – welcome to the new paradigm of our times and welcome to your beautiful life.

Chapter 2

What is a Spiritual Awakening

The First Step

Here we are together on our first step – thank you for saying yes! I absolutely know it is no accident that you have been guided to this book, as I believe there is a part of you that has been asking for another way and wants to wake up from the dream of who you thought you were. That calling is an ancient song of your heart; I promise you your heart never lies, and I also promise you that if you listen deeply, you will receive an abundance of love notes directly from your heart as this process unfolds. They will be delivered in many ways and at different times from many sources and I would, therefore, recommend that you take time to write them down, thus building a journal of insights to inspire and support you along the way.

The more curious and open you are, the more your mind will expand and, in turn, the more inspirational downloads will transpire. These 'downloads', as already mentioned, are very normal when we are tuned into our Source; it will always impart information, guidance and courage for the next step.

I use the term download, because for me, that is literally how they arrive and I have learnt to allow these insights and inspiration to flow through me. In my case they come as a voice/ words in my head, which in this case I have put down on paper, but equally I also follow the loving, guiding voice that inspires me in everyday life. You will come to discover your unique expression of this process, so be open, inspired and ready for the nudges and the 'aha' moments, whether that's as intuition, insights, ideas, hunches, signs, creative energy or the spoken word. As this book unfolds, you will see different ways in which the guidance and nudges arrived for me, and I hope this will inspire you to be open to receiving your own.

You may, of course, already connect in this way as a matter of norm, which is fabulous. Know that this will continue to grow and manifest in many new ways that will surprise and delight you. Either way, I would suggest that you start each day with a childlike innocence, a blank canvas so to speak, along with a willingness to open up your energy field like never before, and be prepared to shed as many old skins as are ready to loosen their hold. Try not to pre-empt or plan how this happens, and notice that if you go into fear or disbelief, it will switch off your connection. This is not about analysing or trying to figure it all out – it is about letting go of what you think you know and literally embracing the unknown. That is where the miraculous occurs and that is where we are heading…

Ultimately when we embrace our SA we will come to a place where our life is completely guided and the 'I know mind' (ego) is gone.

Who, What, Where and Why…?

The start of a Spiritual Awakening can happen to anyone, any age, colour, race, religion or gender – if you have a heartbeat you're a prime candidate! However, not all people will take the path in this lifetime, as crossing the river of change is too hard to comprehend and the familiar feels much safer. Rest assured, you will come to know the truth once you leave your physical body behind, but my question is, why wait until you take your last breath? Why not start living it now? Why wait for the body to break down, why wait for a terminal diagnosis, why wait till tomorrow, next week or next year? The choice is yours.

There is no 'type' per se for those of us who embark on a SA, because at the heart whether we realise it or not, on a higher level of consciousness, we have actually asked for a form (the body) in which to grow and to be part of a collective awakening, which is quickening and expanding like never before. We are a spiritual being having a human experience, and I believe we already signed a soul contract before we were born to experience the many diverse ways that can only be felt and seen from within a body.

In a body we are seen as individuals, coming from different backgrounds, cultures, circumstances and family dynamics. We may live in a rich, affluent country with a Maserati parked in the garage. We may be living in poverty, dragged up in the gutter, Mr and Mrs Average trying to get by and toe the line living a perfectly conventional life, or we may have gone totally off-piste and rebelled against tradition and normality. It matters not, because as you will discover, beneath the human persona there is something far greater waiting to emerge if we are willing to allow it. You are NOT the odd one out or an exception – everyone at their core has this fundamental divine spark within them and it is the driving force wanting us to WAKE UP and express only LOVE!

In summary, folks, each one of us has the potential for a SA – it's whether we hear the calling and decide to change or not, that determines its unfolding!

Moving Beyond Words and Labels

The first question I asked in the interviews I conducted was: What does a SA mean for you? Without exception, the answer when distilled down was the same for everyone: "It's about coming home to who we really are." This is a short, but sweet, summary and very accurate, but I guess the question on your lips may be, what does that really mean and who are we coming home to? Those who have found 'it' don't need an explanation as it is a deep knowing, but how then to put that indefinable 'thing' into words?

When I was first told I was having a SA, I didn't have a clue what it meant and, most certainly, did not see myself as spiritual in any way. In my naivety, I thought that being labelled spiritual meant I would be religious or belong to a holy order or group. It took me some time to move beyond that particular false premise, and that is why I want to demystify all these labels to help you understand what it's all about.

When I asked the powers that be on my iPhone, Siri (other phones are available), what the word spiritual actually meant, the answer was: 'affecting the human spirit or soul as opposed to material or physical things'. In other words, our spiritual self does not have an identity attached to it, whereas most humans have a very strong physical identity and personality, which has been cultivated over many years. This persona, be it our name, gender, job, political leaning, family history, culture, hair colour, education, history or financial status, etc., has become hardwired due to repetitive behaviours, observations and commentary that we received as we were growing up. This became a subconscious programme which we carry into our adult life.

Our spiritual being is the opposite – formless and with no need for an identity. You do not have to have a particular faith, religion or philosophy to be spiritual – it's part of your natural way of being and just because it's a label called 'spiritual' should not define you either.

By its very nature, there is no exclusive club to belong to in the formless energy field and it is certainly not exclusive or discriminating in any way. It is a vast boundless mass of spaciousness in the quantum field of potentiality. This space, by its very nature, can't be seen or held, so in reality it's nothing, but in truth it is everything – and I mean everything. I know this is a paradox, but to the human limited egoic mind we have to start somewhere as we begin to make sense of the formless. It's a bit like the essence of a flower or a beautiful sunset – you can't put it in a box or hold on to it and stick it down somewhere; it can only be experienced in the moment as a feeling, and attempting to define in words is almost impossible.

This can be a stumbling block for many because we want to

be able to make 'it' tangible and measurable, and in a world where we have been taught to see it before we believe it, it just doesn't cut the mustard. But I am asking you to believe in 'it', be less of the critic and get ready to see it manifest in a multitude of ways, which will leave you without any shadow of a doubt that 'it' is real.

Man has many names for this essence/energy, and as already intimated, words don't do it justice. One word, however, that was helpful for me in the early stages of my SA was the word Love. I use a capital 'L' here, as the Love I am referring to is not a sentiment or a form of romance. It is a vast, intelligent force that spins our planet in its orbit, creates the gravitational pull to keep us from floating out into space, beats our heart, creates new life, turns an acorn into an oak tree and human potential into matter. And this, dear friend, is what we are beginning to tap into when our SA unfolds. It's always been there, but for most of us, we separated from it partially or fully in our formative years.

This supreme Loving power is always with us and calling us to a life of unlimited joy, ease, abundance, well-being, contentment and deep inner peace. Like it or not, you are part of it all, and once you accept this, life will really start to take on a delicious natural flow and new direction. But before the flow, we have to address the mediocre trickle that most of us accept in our lives and be willing to open up to the magnificent torrent of LOVE that just wants to keep on giving.

An Adventure of a Lifetime

As one of the explorers who found themselves 'accidentally' on this voyage, I discovered that the path to realising this Love was not always straightforward or without its turbulent times. In the early days I had no map, compass or sextant to guide me and, as such, found the voyage of uncharted territory extremely frightening and overwhelming. Not only was I running blind, but I had to learn to pilot the ship, acquire new skills to ride the waves and find a safe passage through the tsunamis, undercurrents and raging storms.

At times I would have been happy to have crashed on to the rocks into oblivion, but somehow, I made my way to a safe harbour, where I found some respite along with a crew to accompany me on my continuing journey. These mighty companions had many skills and insights that I would need to make the journey more pleasant and palatable. I was then given many gifts: maps showing new territory, boundless provisions and eventually a certainty of my destination to lands of plenty, paradise islands and vast treasures.

I didn't choose the journey consciously, and I often wondered if it was all the Enid Blyton books that I had read as a child manifesting in this adventure of a lifetime! I was always in awe of the adventures that unfolded on the pages of those books in my youth and I would lose myself for hours on end. It was a magical time of innocence and delight, and like all good books, there is part of us that doesn't want it to end, leaving us sad when the last page is turned. But, thankfully, I have learnt that there is always a new adventure book awaiting us when we are ready for the next phase in the infinite cosmic library.

Redefining and Rebooting

Before we go on, I feel it's important to redefine this Love that I speak about, whilst getting transparent about the small love that most of us believe is normal. We need to reboot our minds just like we reboot our computer and start afresh. So, let's redefine this 'small' love. It has had thousands of songs written about it, with themes of romantic love, lost love, unrequited love, heartbreak, abandonment, endings and suffering, to name but a few. It seems that this love hardly ever lasts and is changeable, resulting in a desperate attempt to save it, hold it, shape it or define it, in some whimsical, crazy way. Yet, under the surface of this small love is fear, and this is why so many people are afraid, cynical and certainly wary of opening their hearts to it. I mean, it is no surprise that we would be on our guard, and controlling, manipulating or watching our back, just in case it's going to hurt us, or even worse, be taken away from us. It's not surprising then, that so many are trying, in vain, to mould it and make it perfect in some way, with weary cries of: "If you loved me, you would/wouldn't do X or Y to me – you would do A or B to 'make me happy'!" And so, we get lost in an ever-decreasing circle of dissatisfaction, control, blame, judgement and grasping. Some become addicted to it, whilst others are disdained by it, and we go on to create a whole story around what we think this love is – it becomes corrosive, dysfunctional and quite often codependent – none of which are particularly a barrel of laughs!

But rest assured there is some very good news – phew! The True Love that you are in the process of awakening to, is beyond the body, beyond words, beyond time, beyond limits and is there for you 24/7 without exception. On top of that, it has no conditions in which it will stop, and it is not keeping score, looking at the past or judging you for any misdemeanours you feel you may have done or not done. It is incapable of judging, condemning or labelling anything as good or bad. It is not here today and gone tomorrow. It doesn't end when you leave your body, and will continue as you ascend into the non-physical, where you will be at one with it for eternity.

To put that into some kind of perspective I would like to invite you to Andromeda, earth's largest and closest galaxy, which, if you wanted to pay it a visit, would take you some 2.537 million light years. Now, you have to admit that's quite a long way, and to be honest it kinda blows my mind when I try to even begin to think how vast that space is. Just close your eyes for a moment and try to imagine the magnitude of what we are talking about here – it's pretty damn vast! And if you're in the know, when it comes to outer space and all things quantum, you will be aware that there are also many, many more galaxies beyond that, not to mention black holes and the space beyond space.

You may be wondering why the heck I'm rambling on about all this space stuff – well, it's so you can open up to the concept of this vast spaciousness, beyond your normal space in time within a body, which is just a hint of how much Love there really is 'out there' – it's boundless and is what our heart is yearning for.

Another word many use is God, and I want to say right here and now that it's certainly not a man sitting on a cloud watching your every move, ready to condemn you and send you off to hell if you commit a perceived sin. No, not at all. It is a supreme eternal expansion beyond anything our mind can even comprehend, where words and the logical brain are required, quite frankly, to take a back seat. It's a visceral colossal vastness, which to quote our friendly superhero Buzz Lightyear is, "To infinity and beyond"! And what's so cool, is that you are part of that infinite vastness – yes, you! I hope you're beginning to get a little excited at the prospect of finding out more about this infinite Love?

The older I am, the less words I have to describe 'it' – it is less defining not more defining. It's an absolute and unshakable knowing of stability, security, joy, expansion, love and safety. I feel the three-letter word of God is too small to describe 'it'. It is non-verbal.
Sarah Cox[3]

Defunking God

I feel this is a really important time to bring God fully into the picture, so we can begin to dismantle the monumental misconceptions that have been built up for so many, and shake up the old ways in which we see this dude/dudes! This three-letter word, God, is what man has used to describe the indescribable in some shape or form for millennia. Unfortunately, many people get their knickers in a twist and want to prove the rightness or wrongness of God, they want to fight to prove it or disprove it, they want to obliterate those who don't agree with their way of thinking and they can use an extraordinary amount of time and energy trying to make their way – the only way.

In creating this three-letter word and all its offshoots in the form of approximately 4,300 religions, all of which have their own names and set of rules for living, man has, in actual fact, created separation. I believe that this separation is the ego's way of keeping us disconnected from the infinite Love that I described earlier.

Inevitably these man-made religions have attracted many people, and most of them well meaning; however, over time the original essence of the meaning of the Love behind the God of their particular religion has been distilled – a bit like Chinese whispers... Eventually this results in walls and impenetrable fortresses being built to keep each group safe and secure. This 'them and us' scenario has a vast ripple effect resulting in different camps of believers, non-believers and in-betweeners. God has now become so loaded, that the true Divine Love behind it has unfortunately been distorted and categorised into different boxes, thus hiding the real truth, and blinding the masses, who at heart just want to get along and unite.

I am not saying there is anything wrong with religion and I know that it serve many people in a wonderful way and does bring people together in Love – so this is not about condemning religion per se, but it is about highlighting how it can divide groups of people, and my intention is always about uniting people and opening hearts – not closing them.

I shut down from God and religion in my teens, and grew to have a shedload of resistance around the God word! In fact, I used to have a visceral bodily reaction, which would literally make me cringe, wanting to turn away with great gusto from whoever was on the God vibe. Basically, my agenda was 'get me out of here'!

Back then I was under the impression that God was a religion and a religion was certainly not what I wanted. Don't get me wrong, I didn't have a problem with anyone who had a religion at all, and I still don't, but I did not, under any circumstances, want to be indoctrinated, preached to or converted.

I can remember the time when I consciously switched off and rejected religion. I was in an RE lesson in secondary school. It was one of those moments in the classroom when I was trying to look attentive and interested (you know those moments), yet every fibre of my being just wanted to be somewhere else – anywhere but listening to this religious mumbo jumbo. Looking out the window and daydreaming of playing hide and seek, skimming stones or losing myself in my latest Enid Blyton adventure was a whole lot more appealing, but there I was trying to listen to the teacher and take in information that just didn't inspire me in any shape or form – not really a winning combo!

You see, back then I was a realist, a staunch 'prove it to me, or I'm not interested' kind of a girl. I was very black and white and actually quite happy with my own interpretation on life, thank you very much. But somebody, somewhere back in the day decided that RE would be a compulsory part of education, and didn't really realise how it would actually backfire for hundreds of thousands of bright kids who realised they had a mind of their own and, as such, should be left to make up their own evaluation of this guy called God and the 'bigger picture'.

Hearing about the Virgin Mary, how water was turned to wine and how Jesus was nailed to a cross, didn't really turn me on and, of course, wasn't exactly in line with a realist! But what really nailed if for me (sorry for the crucifixion metaphor – but it seems kinda fitting here) was how could a 'loving God' exist, as I personally witnessed so much pain and suffering in the world.

It was the mid 70s and the Northern Ireland troubles were rife, and unless you lived under a stone, you could not escape the images of cruelty, hatred and brutality presented on TV on a daily basis, as well as in the press. It upset me deeply, as did any injustice and war in the world. I could not understand why people would do this to each other and certainly could not fathom how a 'God' would let this happen. Nah – I was done with this religious crap and switched off – full stop.

In my innocence and subconscious need to protect myself, I wisely took the path of least resistance, which was to focus on things that made me feel happier and were more palatable to my young taste buds, than all that craziness I perceived out there. I realised there was nothing I could personally do to change what was happening in the world; it all just seemed too big and overwhelming for little old me. But the one thing that did give me comfort, was knowing that I could be a good person, a kind person and do the best I could in my life. I saw a vision in my mind of a pebble being thrown into the water, with myself as the pebble, and the ripples were the effect I could have. I knew that these ripples had the potential to touch others and that felt like a good thing to me. So, I decided that that was the best I could do, and hoped that this would be enough in some small way.

Thankfully, my parents were also disinterested in religion. My father was a very proud atheist, and often declared that when he died, he wanted to come back as a dog (having our own family's pampered pooch – I could see how this was quite an appealing option). My mother never really talked about religion or went to Church, but she had her own thing going on, which was never spoken about, but looking back, was quite a healthy, non-attached way of being. She did, however, particularly love the hymns and songs found in religious services and I think, like many, she enjoyed the comradery and community that was present in many churches and I can see why it is so appealing for those people who want to belong to something.

I am grateful that my parents gave me the gift of making up my own mind and didn't push me in any particular direction regarding religion, but one thing my parents did encourage me to do, was to read newspapers and 'educate' myself in the goings-on of the world. I did give this a go, trust me I did – but again, I had absolutely no interest whatsoever in 99% of what was being portrayed in the media and decided that it just wasn't for me either – a bit like Ski yoghurts and instant coffee – try as I might to look educated and refined, you just get to the point when you say, enough is enough! So, God, along with newspapers, instant coffee and Ski yoghurts were confined to the bin – slam dunk! I was now in the non-believer camp, and without realising it, had also separated from the possibility of having a relationship with this God/Love/Source and Supply – all because I saw God as a religion. Having spoken to many people about this subject, I know I am not alone in this switch off process.

Later, much later on my SA journey, I would discover that everything I saw in the world was just a mirror of my own unhealed mind, and the ego's ploy of keeping me and everyone else separated.

The separation, that results from all the associated different beliefs about God, is the opposite of what our hearts really want. All of us, whether we admit it or are even conscious of it, want to feel we belong, and are accepted and loved for who we are. Our true self wants to be encouraged, inspired, creative, playful, thriving and free flowing. Anything else is excruciatingly painful, and I believe that this separation has now become the dis-ease of our time, and causes a lot of pain and suffering – and what do we do when we are in pain? We project it on to others (subconsciously, of course), thus creating not only a war within, but without too.

Any form of war (attack or defence, which by the way doesn't have to be just physical, but can be in words and thought too) comes from an energy of fear and could not be further from who we really are. This fear may be disguised and projected in many ways, with layers of hand-me-down baggage, dramas and false projections, manifesting in numerous behaviours, habits, condemnation and complaining. This is the opposite of True Love.

Whatever moment that we start to get curious, ask the bigger questions or get to the point when we fall to our knees and decide that enough is enough, is when we are ripe for potential change and the beginning of our SA – because when we ask, it is always given. But we have to get silent enough to hear the answers, and if we are serious about change, then the work can begin.

What is God/Universe for you?

I can't define it but I feel it as energy. Those feelings of upliftment, a sense of confidence, being in flow, essence of trust, being able to fall back and know something will catch me. I feel it in nature the most, with animals, art, teaching, everyday living and I feel we need to relax into it and stop trying to get it. The more you become aware of it the more it will be there for you.

Gabrielle Anya Rafello[4]

That Three-Letter Word

If you eventually want to be free and find peace, it can be incredibly useful to do a check-in around your relationship with this three-letter word. This kind of enquiry is pretty important work, and can gently help uncover any hidden beliefs or resistance that may be running the show.

Take a moment to just notice what your story is around God. I encourage you to do this with an open heart and childlike, curious innocence. Take a few conscious breaths, soften your body and bring to your awareness any images, words, feelings, judgements, beliefs, fears, resentments or blame that maybe bubbling beneath the surface.

Jot down what you discover.

You may feel some uncomfortable feelings in your body. If so just breathe and be mindful of where you feel them. Do a gentle body scan from your toes, up to the top of your head and get a sense of any pain, tightness or blocks that you notice. Take your time, the ego will want to skip this altogether, but it's so important to get present and real with what you are feeling. This may be a new practice to you or something you have done before; either way trust the process and be open...

You may also want to zone out so be aware of any numbness that arises. This is quite common and a natural coping mechanism, because in the past it was too unbearable to cope with the pain or hurt we experienced. Don't get caught up in the mind's chatter or feel you need to have an answer, just allow whatever comes up to be revealed to you, and trust that this is a good thing and you don't need to run away from it anymore.

Allow your breath to be directed to those parts of your body where you feel the resistance, and just be there in the present moment. You don't have to try and fix or change anything. Just breathe and focus on allowing more spaciousness to arrive in those places. Feel how that spaciousness can grow and extend with each breath that you take. There is no rush, just breathing, noticing and allowing.

Once you have done that for as long as feels comfortable, begin to form a picture or awareness of who or what you believe God to be. This is so important if we want to be free of fear and limitation, because it can help you recognise your subconscious beliefs.

I'm not going to say that this enquiry is always easy – it can feel challenging as we start to uproot our old conditioning, but I feel it is healthy and vital to our personal growth, and to developing a fresh and clean approach to God.

Some of you may already have a healthy relationship with

the God of your understanding. Celebrate this and take some time to appreciate your connection by writing down all the emotions, feelings and joy you feel, and take this opportunity to deepen your relationship. I encourage you also to invite more Love into every area of your life, especially if you feel some past hurt, trauma or loss is still blocking you in some way. There is always relief and healing when you are willing to open your heart and release these issues.

Either way, you can, if you wish, say a prayer or vow to free yourself of anything that has separated you from the big Love that no longer serves you. You may find one of these suitable – please tweak any of the wording to fit what resonates with you and trust that your prayer will be answered.

God, I pray to undo the blocks to your awareness and accept you as my infinite supply. Please help me forgive my old grievances and false beliefs that you are punishing, condemning or absent from my life. I desire to know your LOVE. Thank you.

I vow to open my heart and let the light of Truth transform my fears or judgements around religion, so that I may come to know the Beloved. I am open to your guidance and healing – I am willing to let you in. And so it is.

I pray to the God (put in the name that works for you here) of my understanding that he/she/it will show me the truth and help me release any old and worn-out beliefs that are blocking my true self to shine and that this is done for the highest good of all. Thank you.

To the LOVE that created me, I ask that you reveal to me my true beauty and magnificence and help me to connect to the depth of joy that is waiting for me and to be expressed through me. I pray for the light of my soul to be expressed through you and that I am guided on how to share this in the world. Amen.

Sit quietly and allow your whole body to deepen into the now, and trust that you don't have to go anywhere and that you will be guided and supported on your next step. This is called faith and we have to get out of our own way and let God guide us in his perfect way, in the perfect timing and always under grace.

In my experience this process is not a quick fix; it's the opening of a doorway into places that have, understandably, been hidden and buried away. It's a bit like an old library that has been in a time capsule, untouched or unvisited for many years, with layers of dust and cobwebs building a ghostly film. Your mind is no different, and I am sure you understand how liberating it can feel, when we eventually do a spring clean and discard what is no longer relevant. It can feel so cleansing and cathartic with a new sense of excitement, as we look forward to discovering new treasures to fill our bookshelves, which are more in alignment with our current life.

I hope that this process has helped you in some way or shown you your deeper fears about letting God into your life, but if you are still having trouble with the God word, I find that using another word like Universe, Love, Higher Self, Infinite Intelligence, Beloved, Angels, Cosmos, Friend, Great Spirit, etc., etc., softens everything. So please use whatever word works for you, and remember it is just a word and you give it all the meaning it has. Be mindful and willing to let go of your old stories around God and start to trust in the BIG Love that's behind it. With this willingness you will find the way, the word, the knowing that resonates for you. In Love there is no guru or superior way – we are all equal, we are all from the original Source.

Throughout this book I will intersperse different words for the big Love, as I know the God word may still be challenging and I don't want to block your SA just because you are not happy with the God word being used. I will also continue to offer you opportunities to dismantle or review your beliefs, thinking, programming and conditioning. This will be done in various ways that I have found beneficial, not only for myself, but for clients I have worked with. In my experience building a set of tools that helps us along the way is of such value. It gives you the opportunity to try different things and decide on which ones you want to keep handy and keep in good working order in your toolbox!

Chapter 3

Who Are You?

To move forward on our journey, it's helpful to uncover our old identity to find our true identity. These identities have been disguised as a multitude of habits, beliefs, projections, constructs and perceptions. These blind spots, by their very nature, are out of view, but if we are dedicated to this path of truth and SA, we can begin to dismantle them. If, however, we feel we 'know it all' already and blame everyone and everything else for the cause of our suffering, it will be a slower and more painful journey. Trust me, I know this first-hand as it took me several years to see this hard wall of protection around myself, before I could really begin to get clarity and peace in my heart.

The dismantling and timing involved takes what it takes, so it's helpful to let go of an end date or completion time and instead just enjoy the ride. I had to learn to let go, trust and build a relationship with this new way of living, and once I surrendered the time frame, the easier it became and the more I could actually embrace the beauty of life.

These days I like things to be as simple as they can, I am less interested in proving anything and have made a commitment to myself to be as open, authentic and innocent as I can.

Seek not to change the world, but choose to change your mind about the world.
A Course in Miracles[5]

Ego vs Love

I would like to give you a little clarification on the meaning of ego:

In Freudian and Jungian terms, the ego is the awareness and

the framework of your individual being, i.e. your ideas, beliefs, ideologies, social desires and fears, which builds a world of perceptions and assumptions. Spiritually, ego (edging God out) is the veil of the personality/identity that uses the body for pride, pleasure and attack to keep you separate from your Source and the Universal oneness.

This simple, yet clear list shows the illusion/learnt identity and its opposite, i.e., The Truth.

Who we think we are (Ego)	Who we really are (Love)
A body	A spiritual being
Fear	Love
Darkness	Light
Limited	Unlimited
Someone that can die	An eternal energy being
Something to prove	Nothing to prove
A victim	Innocent
In survival	Thriving
In lack	Abundant
A life of drama	A life of peace
Control	Trust
Guilty	Guiltless
In time	Eternal
Separate	Whole
Defended	Undefended
Suffering	Joy

The differences can be quite striking when we first see them, especially if this is a totally new concept, and it may bring up some unease or confusion, which is totally normal and to be expected, but I can only reassure you that with your willingness to change and 'wake-up', you will be able to find a way to move from a fear-based identity to a natural way of living in utter joy, peace and Love.

I lived my life pretty much from the left column for many years – I did dip into the other side, of course, but my default was set to fear as my primary way of coping in the world. Eventually I started to understand that I had been lost in the material world of form and very well trained by society to revert back to the place of distrust with the 'watch your back mentality', which ultimately led me to try and control most things in my life, to make sure I was safe – the classic ego construct!

I hope you are feeling the pull to column two, and ready to ditch column one, once and for all. I can assure you it will end the internal and external war. There will be a lot that needs to fall away before one is constantly living in this new paradigm, but rest assured that this is where the SA is leading you.

Joseph Campbell calls this the hero's journey, which involves various stages to reach the elixir.

This journey can be seen in many movies and books, which shows us how light overcomes darkness, good overcomes evil and love overcomes hate. There is no surprise that so many descriptions of this journey have been shared in this way, and we can relate to the hero finding their way home. Some examples of this are in: *The Matrix, The Wizard of Oz, Star Wars, The Lion King, Harry Potter and the Philosopher's Stone, Superman,* etc., etc., and it's no different for us as we embark on our own SA. Our own initiation is awaiting us and the chances are there won't be fireworks, a party or a round of applause at the end of it, but what there will be is a deep knowing and contentment, as well as a heart that is wide open and ready to share the joy everywhere it goes. We will be able to give away what we have learnt and stand strong like a beacon, lighting the way and giving hope to others. I'm a real sucker for those who have walked the walk and come out the other side. It showed me that if the 'ordinary' person could do it, then so could I, and it's no different for you either.

The rest of this book will give you examples, insights and clarity of the SA Journey, i.e., your own hero's journey back home and it can be summarised in this way:

- The ordinary world (Asleep/separation from Source)
- Trying to conform, fit in and follow the way of the ego (Fear)
- A sense of disillusionment emerges (Pain, trauma, unease, dissatisfaction)
- Questioning (Is this it? What's gone wrong? Why isn't it working?)
- Struggling to find peace (Keeping the status quo)
- The call to adventure/truth (Breaking point)
- Falling apart (The dissolving of the ego identity starts)
- The dark night of the soul (Facing our inner demons)
- Initiation (Stepping into the unknown)
- Asking for help (The mentor, ally, way, guide appears)
- Hope and new vision (The desire of your heart becomes clearer)
- Purification (Conscious mind training and learning to forgive)
- Trust (Opening to your Higher Power as your supply and sustenance)
- The road less travelled (Your purpose unfolds)
- The elixir is revealed (Know thyself)
- The homecoming (A life of surrender, grace, flow, faith, prayer, love and joy)
- Freedom (I Am)
- Shining your light (Extending the love – walking with mighty companions)

Let us begin...

Chapter 4

How It All Starts

This wake-up call can manifest itself in a variety of ways. For many, it starts as a feeling of just not belonging or a hunch that something isn't quite right. This builds over time and can eventually manifest as a breakdown, burnout, traumatic event, illness, terminal diagnosis, relationship breakdown, addiction, abuse (self or another), constant stress, fear or some drama or catastrophe. We may or may not choose to act at this point or we may just continue down the path in ignorance or denial with a 'better the devil you know' mentality or a stoic persona that everything is okay and we must just knuckle down and just get on with it. It can feel safer that way and somehow very familiar, but in reality, this well-trodden path begins to feel like we are carrying a heavy lead weight, which is far from a walk in the park and certainly not in the direction of peace and joy.

Slow and Steady – For many it is a slow drip by drip eating away of the soul, like the hard limescale in your kettle building up over a period of time, causing an unsightly and foggy residue. This slow burner seems to go unnoticed for the most part, but eventually, if we are not conscious enough to recognise what is happening, it will build up and reveal itself in a multitude of ways – from unease, anxiety, fear, stress, depression, poor health, sadness, grief, disharmony, cynicism, dissatisfaction, control, unhealthy relationships, inferiority or bouts of anger. It festers away like a septic boil, ready to pop at any time. We hold it all together for years, living the same old life in the same old way, but the inevitable happens as the toxic boil eventually explodes, spewing its contents everywhere.

Wham – The BIG bang! This may arrive for those with a relatively happy disposition in life, who are managing quite well thank you very much, but are hit by a tsunami which shakes their world, and in many cases, turns it upside down. This wake-up call is knocking at the door in a loud and profound manner, screaming for your attention!

A Bit of Both – This is a combination of the drip by drip festering away, as we keep the stiff upper lip holding it all together, because that's what we are supposed to do – right? We ignore the signs, bury our head in the proverbial sand, make the best of it and keep on going. But eventually the Universe will deliver something to shake us up and wham, bam the tsunami hits seemingly 'out of nowhere' and brings us to the only logical place – our knees!

My own experience was a bit of both. I was most definitely the one who kept everything safe, wore the mask of perfection very well and had no desire to rock the boat in any shape or form. In reality I was holding on for dear life and clutching the tiller with such pressure that my hands were turning blue and my jaw was on lockdown. My well-learned gritty determination of needing to be in control of the destination was actually keeping me blinkered and shut down from anything vaguely joyous, spontaneous or inspiring. And let's be honest, why would I trust the flow, when everything in my life had taught me the opposite. I also had an 'A star' in forward planning, being a step ahead of the game, just in case, and had lost the ability to trust the perfection and beauty of life. One can only live like this for so long until eventually something has to give. The exterior wall has to crumble eventually, because it doesn't have the foundation and deep roots of God to keep it true.

Whichever way it presents itself, the wake-up call will arrive sooner or later, but whether we choose to acknowledge it or not is our free will. For many the safe groove and status quo is easier and, of course, familiar, as the suggestion of any meaningful change is totally excruciating to our controlling egoic mind and to be avoided at all costs! Furthermore, at a biological level, the body is addicted to living in survival mode with a constant barrage of fight or flight stress chemicals surging through it. We become so accustomed to this 'ordinary world', which feels so familiar to us, and in most cases we see everyone else doing just the same, so assume that this is our lot and it's not to be questioned. However, this can only be sustained for so long, and if we decide to ignore the signs and swallow them down, we will inevitably create something far worse in the future.

The physical body will do its best to cope, of course, striving to keep equilibrium and well-being, because that is its job and under the right circumstances it can do this very well. But if we don't listen to our soul, which is relentlessly calling us home, all the stored-up emotional blocks and traumas from our past will inevitably suck the life out of us, resulting in a steady decline of vitality and joy for life.

Most settle for this life of mediocrity in total ignorance and passive acceptance, having no sense of another way. There are those who have an inkling or a spiritual itch that just won't go away, an unsettling gnawing in the gut that something just isn't right, but can't bear to break the cycle and look at themselves. It's bloody hard – it really is, yet this is how most of us have been conditioned to live; I say live, but really it's more of an existence – which is far from a harmonious and inspired life.

Awakenings feel like our heart is breaking and being pieced back together again at the same time. It feels like all the parts of ourselves are at war and they are inviting us to come along for the ride.
Elizabeth Gordon[6]

Some may choose to opt out altogether and take their own life. It's a fast track to the ultimate freedom that we are all seeking. This is quite a tricky subject to talk about, because for many, suicide is the worst-case scenario and we will do anything to stop this happening to someone we know and love. It goes against everything we have been taught to believe by society. But if suicide is the chosen option, I would never see it as a bad thing... and I will tell you why, friends. We are just deciding to drop the body in this world we perceive, sooner rather than later, allowing our soul to return home from whence it came and where we will all eventually go to anyway.

Why would we deny this for someone we love, when ultimately, we want them to be free? It's our own need to keep them here that blinkers our true seeing. We feel it is tragic, unjust, immoral, and that life should be preserved at all costs!! But what cost is it to the person who is suffering, and who are we to say when the right time or the wrong time is for someone to go to the non-physical realm? It is not our decision to make, and to truly love someone we must be willing to let them choose their own path.

This may seem quite harsh to many of you, and I for one used to feel that way too. But I now understand the bigger picture – I know there is no death, because we are not a body (remember the list in the previous chapter). Our soul/spirit, call it what you will, continues, because it is an eternal energy. This is one of the biggest spiritual awakening lessons that we will ever learn, and in my opinion, once we have this one sussed we truly go to another level of freedom.

This does not mean that we are uncaring, and certainly doesn't mean that we want this to happen, of course not, but what it does mean is that we are prepared to trust that it's not our choice. This may take a lifetime to totally accept, and for some it may be a totally unacceptable concept – which I honour and respect completely.

I came face-to-face with this myself with my children, which is, of course, every parent's nightmare and something no one wants to contemplate. I do not wish to go into details, because I wish to respect my children's anonymity, but I can assure you that it felt like my heart had been ripped out, thrown on to the floor and sliced up into a million pieces. But I knew God was giving me an opportunity to let go of my identity as a mother, and see my children as souls and not mine. This has been one of my greatest learnings and has taught me to let go, and I mean truly let go.

I came to know deeply that if this was their path – I had no way of stopping it and at a particularly low point, I received a direct message from Jesus – it was a short, but clear, message that said, *"It's total arrogance to think you have any part in your children's awakening and furthermore, who are you to 'save' them from this crucial learning opportunity on their own journey back home."* I can assure you that it was a real humdinger and triggered all my fears into one massive ball of broken glass in my gut – and yet, I knew this was the truth. I knew that I had chosen my children on a soul level, to help me awaken and learn a crucial lesson, and they in turn had chosen me too. I came to understand the power of Love and acceptance like never before. I also learnt to stop feeling so responsible for their happiness and found a way to Love them and support them, yet set them free at the same time. This resulted in a much healthier and happier relationship for all concerned. They continue to be a great blessing in my life and continue to grow and blossom in their own unique way.

I also appreciate that the subject of death in any form may be very upsetting and disturbing for some of you, and if this is the case, it would be wise to get the right support from someone who will be able to help you uncover and heal this wound.

If you would like to find out more about this subject, I would highly recommend an amazing book by Anita Moorjani called *Dying to be Me*, which will explain to you in a far more eloquent and informative way than I could, that we never truly die. I would also recommend *A Thousand Names for Joy* by Byron Katie, as well as listening to any of the Abraham-Hicks' YouTube recordings about suicide and death. Also, if you truly want a path that will help you uncover the attachment to the body – *A*

Course in Miracles is a masterpiece, as is *The Disappearance of the Universe* by Gary Renard.

The day Bill died was the day that changed my life forever in more ways than one. He had come to peace around dying and somehow, he transmitted that peace to me. It was a bright sunny June day – I knew he was going...
I was on the bed with him and I felt his heart stop and then he stopped breathing. It was just enormously peaceful and I sat with him feeling this peace. I then saw an amazing bright light leaving his body. I was so shocked and didn't know what it meant, but could not deny what I had seen and experienced. This opened a door for me and I wanted to understand what it meant. I started to read about other people who had also experienced the same thing and realised it wasn't as unusual as I had thought. I had indeed been gifted with seeing Bill's spirit leave his body, and I came to know that we are eternal and that Bill was very much still around me.
Annie Campbell[7]

What helped me make sense of this epic topic was understanding energy, because ultimately that is what we all are. Even a seemingly inanimate object such as a chair has a vibrational energy as much as a flower, a star or your heart. Our soul is no different. When the physical body (matter) departs, this energy (wave) continues but in an invisible form to the eye – or so it seems! We are all capable of connecting to this energy field because we are part of it. It's a massive energetic web that links us all, and just like a spider's web when it is touched, it has a reverberation throughout the whole.

We were all born with this innate knowing and natural connection, but unfortunately most of us learnt to, inadvertently, switch it off in our formative years as the ego started to form. And this is where the separation and ego body became the leading role in the movie of our lives.

Not all, though, have switched this connection off and many people are connecting effortlessly to the 'other side' and their loved ones in Spirit. This is not at all seen as the norm, and most people shy away from this subject and see people who connect in this way as a bit 'weird'. Many people just learnt to suppress and hide away what they were experiencing for fear of being mocked or ridiculed. And let's face it, it's not that long ago that these very people were burnt at the stake for hearing voices or having extrasensory powers, and were labelled witches at worst, or mystics at best.

The truth is, we all have access to this energy, no one is 'special' unless we make them so. It's just a case of whether or not we are willing to open up to this natural connection, and when we do, we will know that our loved ones could not be happier, and they certainly do not want us to suffer or spend the rest of our lives living in misery because they are on the 'other side'.

Kids, because they have less baggage and conditioning, naturally sense this energy and talk to their hidden friends all the time or know instinctively that Grandma or Aunty June is around them. But if they are ridiculed or told to stop this 'strange behaviour', they too will be programmed to think that something is wrong, and they then think the same as everyone else and shut it down!

The more people I speak to, the more I realise how many of us have this knowing, but feel uncomfortable to admit it or talk about. It's no different to our natural gut feelings or a sense of just knowing that something is 'out of sorts' or just doesn't feel right. We all have an antenna tuning us into the energy of people, places or situations around us. Once we 'wake up' to this and own it, it becomes so obvious that all energy continues after we die. Furthermore, we come to understand that when the soul leaves its body, it leaves behind all pain, suffering, fear, judgement and hurt. It returns to a supreme Love where pure bliss is experienced and peace rules – so why would we fear this or deny them this quantum leap?

This level of spiritual maturity is a big ask for many of us, and I can honestly say that healing this wound was massive for me. I used to live with so much fear around the prospect of people I loved dying and, like many, became hypersensitive and protective. But happen it did – of course it did, because people dying is the one certainty we all have to face at some point.

My first experience of someone close to me dying, was my father – he had skin cancer, which after several years went to secondary and killed him at the age of 60. His death was actually a relief in the end, as his body went into an inevitable decline, which was very difficult to witness.

The most painful thing for me, however, was being told it was terminal in the first place. I was about 19 years old and remember the total overwhelm of the inevitable – it felt like my whole world had caved in. I felt utterly devastated and out of control, because there was nothing I could do. Not being able to make it all better was overwhelming and crushed me, and I didn't feel able to share how I was feeling with anyone and slowly came to terms with the diagnosis. I got on with life as best I could, and when he subsequently died, three years later, I had completely numbed out and shut down. It was my way of dealing with the pain, and was a perfectly natural way of trying to manage the unmanageable. I later discovered that this is common with many people who are unable to process their grief, let alone talk about it. I wasn't one to turn to alcohol, drugs or seek outside help, so I just got on with it and pushed it all down.

I, like many of my generation, was not taught how to feel, let alone express my inner world. Everyone in my family just swept their feelings under the carpet of safety and normality and, of course, I learnt to do the same. There is no blame or shame here – it's just something we have inherited from previous generations, and something that is an inevitable symptom, which will sooner or later need to be addressed, if we are to live a life of any meaning.

The real nail in the coffin (sorry, but it fits here) was the death of my brother and his partner in a car accident. By this time, in my late 20s, I had married, had my firstborn and was doing what everyone else was doing in the eyes of a conventional life. I had a loving husband, home and family life. My brother, Steve, and partner, Poushe, also had a young son, Matthew, who was just 14 days older than my own son, Daniel. The difference was, that for Matthew to be born, his mother had to have total bedrest in hospital for most of her pregnancy, and wasn't allowed to put one foot on the floor. This was as a result of already miscarrying four previous babies and physically being unable to hold the weight of the baby inside her. Matthew was, therefore, a miracle and, as you can imagine, a very much loved and longed-for child. Every one of us was overjoyed at his arrival and his parents could not have been more jubilant with his presence in the world.

When Matthew was just 15 months old, the accident happened not far from their cottage in the Borders of Scotland. Steve and Poushe were killed outright and Matthew survived, but was critically ill. No one knew if he would pull through or if he would be able to live a full life. Against the odds he did survive, although with frontal brain damage. He was eventually adopted by his French aunt in Paris, who brought Matthew up with her husband and three sons. They did an amazing job and Matthew was able to live a good life, albeit with extra support, due to his special needs. I will for ever be grateful for the amazing love and dedication that they had for Matthew, and he developed and grew into the most beautiful and generous soul.

This incident totally crushed me. I could not handle the pain that I felt, and what added more anguish was seeing my mother totally bereft at losing her son, at just 35 years old, in this way.

It was unbearable to witness, and again I couldn't make it all better – I had no way of taking her pain away either, and so the only thing I could do was to push all my grief down to join all the other pain. I was by now building a fortress around me and running on empty. The only thing that got me up each day was the fact that I was a mother to my beautiful baby son; this was my priority and one shaft of light that kept me going. My husband was supportive, of course, but he had needs and wants from his wife, but I had nothing to give him – I was in a void of unimaginable suffering and was barely present in my marriage, let alone the flow of life.

But like all these things, it came to bite me on the bum BIG TIME and that was the day when my life changed forever.

The Falling

It was several years later, and by then I had gone on to have my second child. It was a day like any other day, as I continued trying to keep all the plates spinning in the air whilst trying to be the perfect wife, super woman and super mum to two under-fives – no pressure there then!! In short, life was busy and I was frayed at the edges – but to me, this was just how life was supposed to be, right? Wrong – the Universe had other ideas!

I was in my bedroom doing my frenetic cleaning and headless chicken act, as had become the norm, when a very strange feeling started to descend over me like a heavy weight. I felt like I was standing on the edge of a precipice about to fall into the cavernous black void before me to my death. I was immersed in some altered state, rendering me in a full-on state of high anxiety and fear. My logical mind was searching for something to make sense of, some reference point of what was happening, but there wasn't one. The adrenaline kicked in with all the natural fight or flight responses, such as a pounding heart, extreme overwhelm, shock and feeling utterly out of control. In desperation, I screamed out, "I've had enough, stop this, I can't do this anymore – help me!" – or words to that effect. To whom I was screaming I had no idea, but in those moments of extreme stress and overwhelm you don't think or act logically, something else takes over. And thank God it did, because in that moment I had at last surrendered, I had crumbled and let go. The white flag was now flying!

That moment seemed like an eternity, but was probably only a few minutes in real time, and I was, to put it mildly, shit scared and totally rigid with fear. I didn't like the feeling of losing control one bit, and somehow, I managed to pull myself together. 'Normality' began to kick in, as I was totally aware that the kids were nearby and I needed to be there for them. I had no desire to show my kids that Mummy had lost the plot – no, that just wouldn't do! The stiff upper lip returned with greater stoicism than before and I went back on automatic pilot, shocked and confused for sure, but I carried on and told no one. I tried to forget it had even happened.

In hindsight, I feel it was what is known in the trade as a nervous breakdown – but I was made of tougher stuff than that, or at least that is what I told myself and so carried on regardless. Little did I know, that life would start to change and things would never quite be the same again. It was a long time coming, but I now know, it was the best thing that could have happened to me.

What then started to unfold was a series of events that began a heaven-sent domino effect. The cry for help had been heard, and something bigger than me started to line up the journey of awakening. It was only several years later that I started to see the link and the connection to that event in 1997, and know without any shadow of doubt that 'The Falling' had been the start of my SA.

Chapter 5

The Unfolding Begins

A few weeks after 'The Falling' I found myself looking through the local paper at the adult education evening courses. One particular evening class stood out – I can't remember the exact title, but it was basically an introduction to Holistic/Alternative Health and Well-being. I was curious as I had heard of some of these 'new age' therapies like reflexology, aromatherapy and reiki, but I had no idea what they were all about. I thought, 'why not', what have I got to lose? And so, I found myself on the first evening, totally naive, totally green, yet ready to be convinced. Come on then, I thought, sock it to me. And boy oh boy was I socked to!

At the end of the first class, I sat in total awe of this crazy, mad professor-esk guy, called Dr Ian MacDonald. He was wearing a crumpled grey suit, with slightly wild hair and an air of bohemian eccentricity. He ruffled a few feathers I can tell you, but I loved him. I loved his honesty, passion and wisdom. I wanted to be inside his head and know everything he knew, and I sat there in a daze as I came to the realisation that there was another way to live and I felt like there was a hidden world that no one had told me about. To my surprise, it seemed I was hungry and inspired to know everything I could about this 'other world' and wondered why no one had ever told me about it before. It was a secret that I was now privy to and I couldn't be more delighted.

I subsequently finished the six-week Holistic Introductory course and, with great gusto, signed up for the rest of the six-week blocks that he was running, with themes such as NLP (neurolinguistic programming), vibrational healing and naturopathic healing.

It was like a breath of fresh air. I felt inspired and had butterflies in my stomach at the prospect of this new world. I felt a renewed interest in life and wanted more, more, more... and more I got. (Talk about ask and it is given!) The following year I found myself looking through the local paper again, and this time the page literally fell open, with one particular course jumping off the page. The course was a one-year diploma to train as a Holistic Therapist. I was beyond excited – what, you mean I could work in this field? Wow – I was totally fired up and overjoyed with this potential and, more to the point, so ready to learn something new and something which, at that time, seemed rather radical! My previous work life had initially been in the catering industry and then in my mid-twenties I found myself working as an accounts clerk in an international company, which subsequently stopped when I had my children and chose to become a full-time mum. So, this new direction certainly came out of the blue and was not in the plan, but, of course, I now know, that nothing comes out of the blue!

To my utter delight, I got a place on the course and started in earnest to train in this new world. The holistic/whole person approach just made total sense to me and I really believed in prevention rather than cure, whilst supporting the body in a more natural way. I was the diligent student, and although it was full-on balancing college with family life, I was very happy and determined to see it through. And see it through I did, becoming qualified in Swedish massage, aromatherapy massage, reiki healing, reflexology, basic counselling skills, meditation and anatomy and physiology. It was a shock to the system, but I was so proud of myself for this massive step and became addicted to the learning process. I went on to train in Indian head massage and sports massage in the following year of 2000. It seemed this new decade was lining up some incredible experiences for me, and a few years later, having been so fascinated with the mind (the seed had been planted with the NLP I touched on when I met Ian MacDonald), I went on to train as an NLP Practitioner and Integrated Hypnotherapist.

I now had a great set of qualifications and tools in my toolbox. I was on a mission to heal the world and wanted to make sure that everyone understood what this stuff was all about. I came to realise that even though this grandiose vision was mixed with great passion, it was also mixed with my, as yet unknown, codependent desire to fix a perceived broken world. I would eventually come to discover that there was nothing to fix and the outside 'broken' world was but a projection of my own unhealed mind.

But that was my reality back then and the new-found passion spilled out into my awakening world and, as a result, I started to meet new people with different ideas and philosophies. I was being initiated into the spiritual world and soon discovered a new creed of people. I have to say it was somewhat overwhelming and totally radical and, to be honest, I had no idea of what spiritual really meant. I just went along for the ride.

I was on a fast track to the next level of learning. A new world was unfolding before my very eyes, eyes which were now big and wide! Life just kept opening up, taking me to new experiences, people, books and the metaphysical world. Over those few years everything in my personal development just went up a gear, whilst my family life trundled along in the background. I loved my children and husband dearly and was trying to be the best I could, but cracks were by now appearing in my marriage. Like good people, we tried to keep it all together and fix it in conventional ways, such as counselling, but it just didn't get to the core of what was really happening. This I discovered several years later, but for now we just kept going and doing our best.

The Universe really started to point me in a new direction in terms of my SA, guiding me to new environments and people, and through a series of 'coincidences' in 2003, I found myself starting a psychic development group at my local healing centre.

This was not something I had been looking for I can assure you, and had absolutely no idea what all this 'weird stuff' was about, but this just seemed what happened to me at that time in my life. One thing after another would keep presenting itself and I just kept saying yes!

I had entered a world that was about to loosen up my mind and shake off old limiting beliefs like nothing before. I started to feel energy, see colours, images, people and hear voices – oh crumbs, I was becoming one of the 'weird ones'! But I didn't care, it felt good and I felt alive, I was starting to connect to another world which felt strange, yes, and out of my comfort zone for sure, but something just kept me hooked and wanting more.

As I learnt to trust this process, I really began to enjoy this new level of feeling, seeing and hearing through different sensations, eyes and ears. I was connecting to a much higher vibration than just this physical world and, being one of those people who needed to experience things first-hand, I knew with great certainty that my own experiences were real and I couldn't argue with what was happening. The energy that started to move through me in those meetings made me giddy and, at times, I had to literally hold on to the seat as my body recalibrated. In the past, this type of strange happening would have had me running for the hills, but deep within me, I knew this was something positive and I was in awe of the messages and insights that were naturally coming forth in the group and through me.

It really showed me that when the student is ready, whether they realise it or not, the teacher or experience appears. This was happening more and more, and on one hand I loved it, but on the other hand part of me still just wanted to be normal, and most normal people were not connecting to the spirit world and dimensions beyond the material plane! I hid in the proverbial closest and didn't want my family or friends to think I had lost the plot completely and only shared it with a few other weirdos just like me!

Falling Apart

After a couple of years my confidence grew and I soon felt ready for change. Something inside just knew that I had outgrown this group, although I wouldn't have been so bold to have expressed it in that way at the time, as that felt quite arrogant to the ego mind. I had to accept that life was taking me constantly in new directions and I was now learning to trust that journey.

Low and behold, within a few weeks of feeling like I wanted to move on, a 'chance' meeting with someone I vaguely knew led me to a meditation group just minutes from my home. I was given the name of the lady who was starting up this new group – her name was Sarah Cox. I rang her up, she asked a few questions, and before I knew it, I was walking through the door on the first evening, along with a dozen or so other people.

I remember so clearly, Sarah asking each of us in turn to share why we were there and what we were looking for, and I felt some relief in expressing how I had been feeling. I shared that I felt like I was living in two worlds, with one foot in the 'normal' world of family life, husband, home and work, and the other foot in this 'new world' of spirituality, meditation and the like. I had no idea how to merge the two, and I was feeling more and more drawn to the 'new world', yet guilty for doing so.

At this point my marriage was crumbling and, as mentioned earlier, we had tried to fix it, but even though I loved this man and he was my best friend and someone I had intended to spend the rest of my life with, I just couldn't find peace around the disconnect and differences that were showing up in various areas of our relationship. I was growing and exploring new ways in my life, and I felt like I was speaking a different language to him. I felt an overwhelming resistance to his ever-growing (as I saw it then) neediness for me – I felt smothered and stifled and wanted to break free, yet was scared beyond belief of doing so. I was torn and in a constant state of turmoil about what to do – should I stay or should I go? It was really stressing me out, and the constant barrage of trying to work it all out was really taking its toll on me. I felt like I was going insane, and the armour that I had previously built for protection was beginning to fall away, and I realised I needed to make sense of it all.

Whilst I was attending the weekly group with Sarah, I found myself longing for more and more of this world. I was feeling a Love and presence like I had never felt before, and in one particular meditation, I experienced a state of pure bliss which was a new experience for me and I didn't want it to stop. On another occasion during a meditation, I also saw myself walking on a beach hand in hand with the love of my life, but it wasn't my husband's hand I was holding, it was someone else's. This was totally enticing in many ways to me and felt very appealing and yet, in reality, scared the hell out of me too, as I knew this was a sign that my heart was ready to meet someone new, which, of course, would result in the end of my marriage. I felt more confusion, guilt and shame, and a heavy dark cloud of despair hung over me that just wouldn't shift.

I knew that changes needed to happen and it began to dawn on me that all those years I had suppressed my feelings were now catching up with me, and that for the last few years I had been trying to fix everyone else, instead of actually looking at my own stuff. Classic codependency as I would later discover!

What I came to understand is that this is a very common trait for many individuals who are trying to deflect their own suffering. It is a form of denial and transference of our own disconnection on to others. A Course in Miracles states, "Beware the unhealed healer," and I realised this was me, and I had come to the point when it was time to look in the mirror, take ownership of my past and start to do the real work and go within. It was not a prospect that felt very appealing, but I knew it was the only way.

Almost on my knees by this point, I went for a reading with Sarah. I was desperate for not only an answer concerning my failing marriage but for a way out, yet in reality totally resistant too. Not a great combination for clarity! What made it worse for me was that I had all the memories of totally and utterly falling in love with my husband when we met. It was the classic Mills and Boon romance and we both adored each other. But 17 years down the line, and even though on paper we had the perfect marriage and we loved each other, there seemed no answer to our problems. Many years later, I would discover the true answer, but I had a long way to go before that came to the light.

As I found myself on the way to see Sarah, I felt deep trepidation, but I knew I had to start this new inner journey somehow, and this seemed like the next logical step. I took a deep breath and gulped down my anxiety as I faced this daunting, yet inevitable, next step.

Sarah was a wonderful healer, counsellor and psychic, as well as channelling Angels (just like I had been learning to do in her groups too), and I felt in safe hands. As she started to tune in and give the reading, she told me that her guides and Angels saw my heart like a stone. I was gobsmacked and shocked at the no bullshit approach – it was straight to the core! These words felt like a knife to my soul, yet a knife that was needed to cut away the armour I had accumulated. Tears started to pour forth like a river breaking its banks. I couldn't stop, and as Sarah continued to offer her channelling, my brother's death came to the surface and my heart began to crack, the façade began to dissolve and the floodgates opened. It was scary and uncomfortable as I wasn't used to being so vulnerable and raw, but my soul was deeply touched that day, because for the first time I had let someone in and, just as importantly, I had truly been seen by someone who loved me unconditionally. My heart and soul wanted to heal, and this was now the new trajectory of my life and SA.

I went home and tried to hide my vulnerability and pain – I carried on being the dutiful wife and mother, but inside I was screaming. Feelings such as rage, grief and frustration were now beginning to come up to the surface and I started to shut down even more from my husband, keeping him at arm's length. He was struggling too and doing his best, and craving comfort from me to soothe his own pain. I was hanging on by a thread and feeling bereft, and I just didn't have the tools or capacity to open up to him and share what was really going on.

The wound is the place where the Light enters you.
Rumi[8]

Breaking Open

A massive turning point for me was attending a weekend retreat with Sarah. It was the first retreat I had ever been on, and was to be the start of many visits to the beautiful centre in Somerset. I was blown away on all accounts and totally out of my comfort zone too. Part of me wanted to run away and yet the bigger part of me knew the score. The Love that I felt that weekend was sublime and beyond words, and I knew the light was breaking open my heart, slowly, slowly. I wasn't ready yet for the full-blown open-heart thing at that point – you gotta be kidding. This was already a massive step for me, but I felt just for a brief moment the comfort of pure freedom and joy, and realised there was no turning back.

A year or so later, the inevitable happened, and my husband and I split up. It had taken a long time for us both to get to this point, and I have to say it was a great relief that a decision had been made, but it was also the worst day of my life too. I was now in unknown territory and it hurt like hell. My heart was breaking, not only from the awakening process, but from losing (as I saw it then) the only man I had ever truly loved, and to top it all I was also going through the menopause at the age of 44. I was on my knees, ripped apart, and fear gripped like a vice with evermore determination, squeezing the last drops of life out of me. I totally fell apart, lived on a knife-edge every day, was acting like a crazy woman, my immune system was on empty, my adrenals were shot to bits and the weight just fell off me. The body can only take so much of being in survival mode like this, and true to form something had to give.

It started with bouts of extreme pain, the like of which I had never experienced – it was off the scale, and I was eventually diagnosed with gallstones. It was no surprise really that the years of repression were now beginning to manifest in the body.

In Louise Hay's book, *Heal Your Body*, she describes how, from the metaphysical point of view, *"in order to permanently eliminate a condition, we must first work to dissolve the mental cause."* She lists a whole array of physical conditions, the probable cause and a relating new thought pattern to help heal it. According to her book, the causes of gallstones are *bitterness, hard thoughts, condemning and pride.*[9]

Gulp – she nailed it!

There was no getting away from it, all the years of unhealed resentment, bitterness, anger and suppressed emotions had now energetically been realised as the gallstones in both my gall bladder and liver, and the point had come when they had now got so big that they were unable to pass through the bile duct. It was a real eye-opener for me and I had a clear understanding, in real time, of the correlation between the mind and body connection. The new thought that I now needed to work with, according to Louise Hay's book, was: *There is joyous release of the past. Life is sweet and so am I.*

I took responsibility for what I had created, understood why it had happened, and was ready to let it go. Even though the well-meaning doctor wanted me to have my gall bladder removed, I knew I could heal it myself and that my gall bladder was an important part of my body, not to be just cut out and disregarded.

I asked the Universe for some guidance, which by now was

becoming more of a natural thing to do, and my answer arrived by way of a book called *The Amazing Liver and Gallbladder Flush* by Andreaz Moritz, which literally landed on my living room table, from a student of the meditation group I was running at the time. I did my research and trusted that this was the way forward for me, and over a period of two years and 13 liver flushes, I released over 100 gallstones. It was quite a journey and, at times, felt quite hard core, but I was determined to heal myself naturally.

As well as the flushes, I continued to release my anger, and came to love and accept my body, particularly my gall bladder. I thanked it for showing me that something was clearly out of balance, and I constantly sent it love, kindness and forgiveness. Again, this is the opposite of what most people do when they are confronted with something like this – they quite often become resentful or upset with the part of them that is causing distress or pain, and are anything but loving towards themselves. They seek a solution outside and expect the medical profession to make them all better, instead of taking ownership of their own dis-ease.

This is really quite radical for many people, but I believe this is the way forward if we truly wish to live a whole and balanced life. I'm not saying don't go to a doctor or have the treatment you need – it can indeed be lifesaving, but what I am saying is, there is another way to look at your body and your well-being.

To this day I haven't had another gall bladder attack, and I am so grateful for that experience, because it taught me to not only truly listen to my body, but to be kinder to myself and heed the warnings before they go on to something far more serious. In short, I was learning to accept and love myself on a completely different level.

Not everyone will manifest gallstones like I did, but I can assure you that our supressed emotions will come out in one form or another – it has to go somewhere!

I continued to address the emotions and feelings that were now beginning to be given a voice, and I realised how out of touch with my feelings I had been. I did this through spiritual counselling, self-enquiry and deep inner work over several years, and it was like learning a whole new language. At times it was agony and I felt overwhelmed again and again, but I was willing to do the work of undoing my past limiting beliefs and stories. My prayer every night was "show me the truth" and I meant it with every cell of my being.

The truth, of course, started to show itself and the old crap surfaced one layer after another. It seemed never-ending, but I had asked for the truth, and what I came to discover over that particularly intense period, is that the ego hates to lose its identity and will do anything to survive, so it comes up again and again with an armoury of guilt, criticism, lack, condemnation, attack, defence, blame, judgement and self-loathing. This stage is different for each person and depends on how much undealt-with baggage we have and, of course, how long it has built up. It is a very normal stage of the SA and, if we truly want to be free and at peace, it can't be rushed, denied or bypassed.

The payoff is totally worth it, friends, and I want to reassure you that it doesn't have to be hard or last for years like it did for me, but I don't want to paint a picture that's all pink and fluffy either and tell you that you can just float your way through it. It really does depend on how willing you are to surrender and trust the journey, and thus why I feel it is so important to be honest with you.

Someone once described this process as the barrel effect. All the years of toxic thoughts or pain produces a build-up of sticky gunge and waste material that congeals and settles at the bottom of the barrel, and contaminates the rest of the liquid. Eventually the barrel gets so full, just like negative emotions in our body, and can't contain its contents anymore and over the edge it goes, but the gunk remains at the bottom, and if it's not cleaned out, will just continue to murk up the rest of the liquid. The only logical thing to do is to get rid of the crap at the bottom, clean it out and then start again. When subsequent liquid is added, it is clear and fresh, and so much easier to keep pure. If any contamination or dirt comes along, it's much easier to clear the scum off before it sinks to the bottom again, thus preventing another build-up. I hope you can see through this analogy, that the benefits of the clean-up operation make complete sense.

The Calling

I was dedicated to the clean-up operation, and continued in this way day by day, week by week, and month by month. Years went by until I began to feel like a different person, and I began to look in the mirror and truly Love the one looking back at me. I started to feel sustained Love, joy and peace for longer periods of time, and there came a tipping point when I knew, without doubt, that I was loved by God. I had learnt that it was only when I turned away from God, that I felt pain and suffering.

Building this relationship with God was the biggest part of the journey, because my relationship with God was at zero point when I started my SA. There were many roads I needed to travel to find this particular truth. Some of the roads led to dead ends, some led me around in circles, whilst others led me to freedom. This happened over a period of about eight years as I continued spiritual counselling, as well as attending a 12-step programme for codependency, studying A Course in Miracles, doing The Work of Byron Katie, understanding the principles of the law of attraction, as well as attending many workshops on self-love, and spiritual practices and philosophies. This particular phase of my SA eventually led me to a pretty radical decision.

You might want to take a seat at this point, dear reader, well I know I did anyway! The decision that I took was to change the whole trajectory of my life, and that decision was to train to be a Multi-Faith Minister. Yes, you read that right, folks, I was guided to become a Minister of God!

From someone who could barely say the word God, to finding myself on the threshold of training to be a minister was indeed a miracle, and was not something I had been looking for, I can assure you. But it just shows that when we let go and trust our heart and soul, we will be led to new opportunities and learning experiences, regardless of what we think we need or want! So how did this radical decision come about?

Sarah Cox, whom I have already mentioned, was by now a big inspiration in my life and I was continuing to work with her, from time to time, as part of my ongoing awakening and healing journey. She had trained to be an Interfaith Minister with the Interfaith Seminary in London and had made friends with a fellow student, Mary Adams. Once ordained they both worked together, and I saw how they had changed their lives in many ways and worked through a lot of their own baggage, and were willing to do the healing. I admired their deep peace and awareness of Love, which had been cultivated in opening up to the God of their own understanding through their training.

I witnessed that whilst they had this deep knowing, they were also 'normal people' and were real, down to earth, yet living, as I saw it, an extraordinary life! This combination was extremely attractive to me, and before I met Sarah and Mary, I had falsely believed that to be a minister of God, one would have to have a religion, be a hermit living in a cave, give up all worldly goods and meditate on a hill for the rest of their lives! But thankfully, I was beginning to see, that this was not the case and 'ordinary' people, just like me, were being guided to step into living a life dedicated to God.

I am among the ministers of God – An earthly messenger fulfils his role by giving all his messages away. The messengers of God perform their part by their acceptance of His messages as for themselves, and show they understand the messages by giving

them away. They choose no roles that are not given them by His authority. And so they gain by every message that they give away.
A Course in Miracles[10]

So how did I come about working for the Big Man upstairs too? I was invited to be a helper at a retreat in Somerset that both Sarah and Mary were running, and was honoured to be asked. I was also overjoyed at the prospect of being part of this kind of work, which had previously seen me on the receiving end. I, of course, said yes and dived in. When it came to the last day of the course, Sarah said to the whole group, "Welcome to our world – this is how we live everyday." As these words landed deeply in my heart, it felt like I was floating in suspended animation, in a complete bubble of bliss, thinking to myself, I want to feel like this every day, not just when I attend a workshop, retreat or meditation. I didn't want to go back home all full of love and light, and then, after a short period of time, feel that emptiness in the pit of my stomach, as life returned back to 'normal' again. I wanted to be free of that dichotomy once and for all, and I wanted to have a sustained level of connection, love and self-acceptance. I was ready for the next phase, and this was a pivotal point in my awakening, and would change the course of my life once again.

Do it trembling, if you must, but do it.
Emmett Fox[11]

Mary had been guided to set up the Vale Ministry to train people to become Multi-Faith Ministers and, up until this point of the retreat, I hadn't considered being part of the training at all. The two-year course was due to start imminently, and if I was going to be part of it, a decision would need to be made soon, and something inside was calling me to step forward and commit to the course. My heart was saying yes, and, of course, my faithful friend the ego was clearly screaming a big NO, coming up with every conceivable excuse and reason why not to.

But this time something felt different, and I knew it was time to take control of my own destiny and be done with the incessant ego downer. I needed a sign, I wanted it pretty damn quickly and I wanted it to be clear. My God, I was getting bold, and true to form, when we ask for a sign with a clear intention, it will be delivered. And that is exactly what happened on that auspicious day.

One of the participants at the retreat asked me if she could work with me, which was unusual in itself as I was just there as a helper, and not really part of the group who were practising their spiritual/psychic skills. A yes came out of my mouth before I could even think about it, and this beautiful lady proceeded to receive a humdinger of a message that I knew had come through from my brother, Steve, in spirit. I can't recall the exact message as I was in a bit of shock, but I felt such a divine love and grace enfold me. It was so affirming and I knew that my brother was giving me a gentle prod!

I had been given my answer and I knew it was time to commit. I knew that if I had gone home and 'thought about it', as was my way, I would have talked myself out of it, so I subsequently spoke to Mary and confirmed I was in! I am ever grateful to that beautiful lady who gave me the reading and the prompt I needed that day.

The die was cast, and on the three-hour journey home, I thought how the hell am I going to pay for it? But by now I was beginning to feel quite cocky, so said to them 'up there' – if you want me to do this training, then you need to sort out the money, because I don't have it! And I left it at that – I was compliantly nonchalant and actually couldn't give a damn either way. I felt like a stroppy teenager, but I kinda enjoyed this new-found rebellion... Mmm what was happening to me.

Within a few days of returning home, I received a message

from a friend of a friend who needed a place to stay after her time travelling abroad. I had a spare room to rent, and this guardian angel arrived in my home and stayed for the exact period of time that I did my training, leaving just one month before my ordination. This more or less paid for the training, and I was beginning to really see the power of the Universe, and the power of asking.

Coming Out of the God Closet

The two years I spent training to be a minister was an incredible insight into my relationship with religion, God and myself. It was not about being a scholar and learning about religion, but about opening our minds and perceptions to the essence behind the titles and words of many of the world faiths. It was about embracing the similarities at the core and, more importantly, what it means to be a devotee of a particular faith and how that shapes an individual's life.

I came to discover a great beauty at the heart of all the faiths we studied and I was discovering that the God I dismissed all those years ago was not at all like the religious interpretation I had been indoctrinated in to. The God I was discovering was beyond words, and I opened up to a plethora of experiences showing me that God was in everything and everybody, without exception, and its Love was all encompassing. I came to remember the truth of who I really was in a much deeper way, and my heart was now fully open to receiving this vast Love. I came to know what oneness really felt like, and I knew that this homecoming was teaching me that this Universal Power was, and always had been, the ultimate healer and elixir of all pain and perceived suffering in the world.

My healing regarding God was massive, and I came to understand that the three-letter word is merely ink formed into shapes on a piece of paper that tries to represent what cannot be put into words. This journey into the heart of Love brought me to a profound awareness of an omnipresent Intelligence and presence that can only be felt, and which eventually becomes a deep unwavering knowing.

Within the training I also learnt how to create and offer ceremonies, such as weddings, funerals, blessings, rituals and healing. This process also really pushed me out of my comfort zone, as I was learning to trust my guidance and create from my heart instead of my head. I had to demonstrate this by presenting my creations in front of my fellow peers and find new confidence and strength based on inspiration from my soul. It was an ineradicably steep learning curve, challenging me to be seen and heard, and shine my light without apology. It was an amazing part of my awakening journey and it culminated in my being witnessed by family and friends at the ordination with my other fellow ministers. It was a deeply moving experience and I was now definitely out of the God closet BIG time!

God didn't hold back, because just one month after my ordination, I was thrown into the deep end with an almighty splash! My ministerial armbands were barely off, when I was asked to officiate my very first funeral service. The panic set in and I wanted to run away and hide, but I had nowhere to hide, and I knew this was now the time to step up and stand strong in my own faith and trust that God was in charge – after all that's what I had signed up to!

It was a big responsibility and a funeral is not something you can get a second run at, you gotta deliver the goods! I had made a vow in my ordination and now it was time to live by it, regardless of my own human agenda. I knew that the only way to do this was to get the hell out of the way and trust that this loving presence I had been cultivating over the last few years would guide me and work through me, and it didn't disappoint. I brought everything together and created a beautiful ceremony, which I feel represented the deceased and the family's wishes. I had to now just deliver it!

When I arrived at the crematorium, I had the collywobbles big time and my knees were knocking, and I thought, why on earth was I putting myself through this! All my old shy and inferior traits were rampaging and wanting to get me as far away as I possibly could get. But I had nowhere to go, I had to face my fears and break the habit of a lifetime. I needed to pull myself together and find a place to be alone for a moment and the only place that fitted that description was the toilet! I was definitely seeing the ordinary in the extraordinary here, but hey a girl's gotta do what a girl's gotta do, and I needed to get my big God pants on and have a little chat with the Big guy... "Hey, man –" I said – "I can't do this on my own, it's too scary, you gotta help me."

I just stepped out of the way and allowed the Divine to work through me. It was all a bit of a blur, but I survived – God didn't let me down, in fact, I felt such a surge of power and presence that it really gave me a boost. I went through the usual ego afterburn, when it pointed out to me how this or that could have been better along with the 'who do you think you are standing up there in front of everyone thinking you are something special' put-me-downs, but I just let the ego have its rampage and felt proud of my achievements anyway.

The main thing that really reassured me was the amazing love and presence I felt from the spirit of the deceased. I felt his energy fill the entire room, and there was no doubt whatsoever that he was clearly at peace, in love and free. I wished everyone could feel this and understand that there is no death, only transformation of energy from matter back to Source Energy.

You see, when people are in grief or fear, there is no possible way that they can connect to their loved ones in spirit, because fear is the opposite vibration of Love. You, therefore, have to lift your vibration and meet them where they really are and hang out in the higher vibrations of love, joy and appreciation. Easier said than done when you are in grief – I understand that so well, but this is the work of awakening, and once we have the awareness, we can then commit to making this our path.

This was a far cry from the old me who lived in fear of death, and I knew part of my calling, on a personal and professional level, was to be able to stand strong in this truth and help support people to also discover this sublime place of awareness. I also understand that grief affects people in different ways, and it can be incredibly hard to move through it and it is, of course, a natural process. But I also know that we don't have to stay in grief for years, and our loved ones in spirit certainly do NOT want us to stay a minute longer than is necessary.

I was so thrilled to have not only conducted my first ceremony, but for also relinquishing my old story of being a shy and unconfident person. I had turned my fear of public speaking into a gift to support others. To be able to stand in front of 50 people, delivering a ceremony of such gravitas, along with holding a space for the grieving, was testament to that turnaround. It just shows that the connection we plug into is greater than we can ever imagine, and I really understood on that day how Love can move mountains and heal the world.

My path was unfolding at a rate of knots, and even though there were still highs and lows and times of despair, I had developed a deep unwavering relationship with my own God. This relationship was key to my next phase of truly living from the heart, and I knew without doubt that this LOVE from Source was now my anchor. I knew I had found what I had been looking for, or more to the point, I was removing the blocks to the presence of Love that had always been there. The Universe was delivering the perfect opportunities for me to heal my old wounds. Serenity and grace were now becoming the norm not the exception.

Chapter 6

Authentic Self-Expression

Life continued to unfold and layer upon layer kept falling away. And on New Year's Eve 2012, I got to the point when I was ready for some play and a new three-letter word – FUN. I put my arms up to the Universe and proclaimed that I was done with the snot, the tears, the tantrums, the pain and the grief, and I was ready to truly live the next phase of my life and wanted 2013 to be very different. True to my asking, the Universe delivered the next phase of my awakening.

As I discovered my new-found verve for life, what unfolded was the awakening of my creativity. This, I later came to discover, was an inevitable result of clearing out the dense old energy and garbage from the past. Once it's gone, it makes way for new energy to flow through us and, of course, this inspired energy needs an outlet. We just have to look at young kids, and see how they are so open and receptive to expressing themselves, whether that be through play, fun, laughter, art, music or dance – they don't yet have a censor or a belief indoctrinated into how they 'should' behave – they are great teachers for us and a reminder that we, too, were once that carefree, and this is what we are returning to on our SA.

It was a delight to find myself on the threshold of this next stage. It also felt a relief from the relentless purging of grief and pain. What transpired was the readiness to express myself and open up to new ways of doing that. This happened first through the voice and a system called The Naked Voice. It was incredibly challenging to start with, as I had been so used to having no voice, and I felt really embarrassed when it came to singing too, but I knew it was time to let myself go. It opened up a space for playing and my teacher showed us all that the voice is an instrument and the world wants to hear it, whether that's as a singer, poet, teacher, facilitator or friend. Wow – this was certainly a different message to the one I had as a child, 'children should be seen and not heard' – I was now ready to turn that particular lie on its head! It was so freeing and liberating – the phoenix was now rising with greater passion than ever before.

I also embarked on 'The Artist's Way' (a wonderful healing process for creativity by Julia Cameron) and spent a wonderful summer opening up to the delights of discovering the hidden depths of creativity that had been suppressed for so long. I was writing poetry, discovering different art mediums and committing to a regular artist's date, and I gave myself permission to try many new things. It was fun and I couldn't quite recognise myself as someone who was creative, but it seems I was mistaken.

Next came the discovery of a form of dance called Vital Danza. This was one of the most profound periods of self-expression that I experienced. I had always loved music and had a very natural ability to feel music in my soul, and dance was always something that felt instinctive within me, but I had never truly explored this medium as a way to connect on a deeper level before. This form of dance was not about learning steps or dancing in a particular way; it was about allowing the music to move and flow through me to allow a unique expression every single time. Sometimes it was flirty, funky and feverish, whilst at other times, it was deep, intimate and gentle. These sessions were always held in a safe space with a facilitator who would guide you but not tell you how to dance, showing their version of each particular set of songs, and you, in turn, would then allow your version to come through you. That could be on your own, with one other or in a group – all the rule books were thrown out of the window! I felt so alive as I learnt to let go of my guarded perfectionism, and at last I felt free to swirl, twirl, leap, scream and play again. It was challenging as I stepped out of my comfort zone many times, but compared to the previous few years of deep grief, this was a walk in the park.

I met some very beautiful souls throughout this time, and opened up to a liberated and authentic community and, in fact, ended up collaborating with my Vital Danza teacher, Helen Thatcher, working together for several years combining the dance with my spiritual teachings in several retreats and workshops. I am so grateful for her and all the many facilitators I met over that period of time – it was a blast!

I was building a life that was so different to my old, structured way and I was falling in love with life like never before. New opportunities and friendships opened up and, of course, there were still times when I had my wobbles, times when I was triggered in relationships, and experiences that would flaw me, but now I had coping mechanisms in place and I took full responsibility for my stuff. I blamed less and less, and took ownership of my own happiness.

One of the other things I also started to do was to travel abroad to retreats and spiritual holidays. This felt very brave and challenging to me as I had never travelled abroad on my own before. I always had my husband by my side, so we made decisions together, which made the process manageable. I had no desire whatsoever to go on a 'normal' package holiday; they just didn't appeal anymore and I certainly would not have gone on my own. But true to form the Universe started to line up baby steps for me and the first trip abroad I took was to go on a Satsang retreat in Spain with a facilitator I already knew. I had attended some of his groups in the UK and I was comforted to know there would be a few people that I would know. This made the process a lot more appealing, but it still brought up some fears and vulnerability related to being unable to speak the language, as well as worry about getting lost or stranded in a foreign country. It didn't stop me though, and all in all this first solo travelling was a good experience.

I started to feel a bit braver, realising that there was a whole world out there waiting to be discovered. It was like a new-found sense of adventure pumping through my veins and I was starting to feel excitement about the world beyond my old comfort zone.

I had been doing a lot of inner child work at that particular time also, and came to discover that this fear, and the need to be in control of my outer circumstances, came from this part of my psyche. I started to notice when I went into wounded or abandoned child in my adult life, which played out in a multitude of ways. It was fascinating, although quite shocking at times, to realise how many of my subconscious behaviours stemmed from this wounded child. I didn't perceive that I had a 'bad' childhood at all and I had felt loved and supported by my parents, but what I soon came to learn was that for so many of us, we do experience upsetting, punishing, belittling and traumatic scenarios in our formative years. This may be experienced within our family, extended family, school, playground, afterschool clubs or just in day-to-day life. Because we didn't have the capabilities or emotional intelligence to deal with what came along for us, we just bumbled along the best we could, either pushing down the experience, becoming withdrawn, quiet and a people-pleaser or behaving in a rebellious, defiant or belligerent way.

My default was to hide, play small and retreat into my shell. I had no ability to express what I wanted or needed, which subsequently results in various forms of defence, justification or victimhood in adult life. Over a period of time, I saw how I carried around these hurts resulting in feeling unfairly treated many times. I would then create relationships and experiences that would mirror the subconscious wounds I had of feeling totally squashed and inferior.

One particular incident that came to light and which I, subsequently, realised had indeed left a deep scar, was when

I was about six years old. It was morning playtime at school, and like all six-year-olds, I was running around and enjoying myself in the playground. Unbeknown to me, a rule had been set whilst I had been off sick from school, which for some reason meant that no one was allowed to play on the grass and it was out of bounds. I hadn't been told this and there were no signs to intimate this either. I found myself running on part of this 'sacred grass' and got caught and summoned to the headmaster's office with a pointing finger of distaste from the adult who spotted me.

I was in total shock, as I had no idea what I had done and took myself off to stand outside the headmaster's office. I felt such an overwhelming feeling of shame, guilt and bewilderment. As a 'good girl' it was unbearable to be standing outside the headmaster's office – this felt like punishment enough for me, but to top it all I deemed that everyone who saw me would be making judgement about the crime I must have committed. It felt like an eternity before I was called into the office, and I don't remember it being such a big deal to the headmaster, but to me it was. It was excruciating, leaving me totally speechless and without the capacity to say what had really happened and proclaim my innocence.

I never told a soul about it as I felt so ashamed and I certainly couldn't have told my parents, as I had no desire to be seen as a 'naughty girl'. I obviously supressed it, blanking it out of my life for eternity, but, of course, it showed up unbeknown to me, in a myriad of behaviours for decades in my life. The reason I want to share this with you is because even though it seemed an insignificant incident to the outside world, it actually shows how deeply wounding these events can be to the tender and innocent soul.

I have seen again and again adults who, to all intents and purposes, are showing up as a 'grown up' in the world, but, in actual fact, are playing out some role from their childhood.

This is not a judgement or criticism, it is just a fact, and once your radar is switched on to this, it becomes very clear when it is happening. It takes great courage and commitment to face this stuff, and more often than not, people just can't see the link from their current life problems or situations to events that happened in their formative years. The ego keeps us believing that it's either somebody else's fault and transfers the blame, or lives in a bubble of perfectionism, believing their childhood was exemplary and their personal character traits have nothing to do with the past assuming that 'that's just the way I am' and, therefore, nothing needs to change.

Let's be radically honest here – we can't change our childhood, but we can change whether or not we stay a victim to it. Yes, it may have been traumatic, abusive or dysfunctional, or it may have been idyllic, dreamy and carefree. But if, in our adult life, we have ever felt pain, suffering, abandonment, judgement, hurt, inadequacy, anger or shame, you can bet your bottom dollar it has its origins in your childhood. It may be very subtle I'll grant you, or it may be glaringly obvious, but either way, it's there to be healed if we are willing to do the inner work. With awareness comes freedom, and I believe that if we truly want to be living a life of authenticity and joy, it is incredibly helpful to look at our family of origins and childhood patterns. Connecting to your inner child can help you break free from the past, and reconnect you to your truth, returning you to your wonderful, happy and natural state of being as an innocent, blessed and beautiful child of God.

Here are some forms of how our wounded child manifests in the adult world.

- Feeling lost or lonely
- People-pleasing
- Swinging from anger to passivity

- Defending and attacking
- Unable to speak your truth or ask for what you want
- Feeling ashamed or guilty
- Judgemental of yourself or others
- Saying sorry all the time
- Self-defeating beliefs and self-talk
- Extra sensitivity to how others are feeling, taking on some or all of their suffering
- Trying to fix others and upset when they don't want your help
- Unable to share authentic love and intimacy with friends, family or partners
- Sexual issues
- Controlling and fearful
- Unwanted habits
- Addiction
- Shyness
- Perfectionism and superiority
- Self-harm

There are varying degrees of how this shows up in our lives, and the ego will want to reject and defend itself with great intensity when these traits start to be identified. I have seen this again and again, and the ego will basically deny everything and blame everyone or everything else as the problem.

When a baby comes into the world, it is totally connected to its Source and full to the brim of Love. It has no identity, judgements or inferiority, it just is... But as the child grows up, it takes on the beliefs, identities and patterns of its environment, the people in that environment and, of course, all the other places it goes to, like school, church, relatives' homes, shops, etc. As we know, a child is like a sponge and this means that because it has no filter, it takes on both the 'good' and the 'bad', and before you know it, it starts to form its own ego identity and so it goes on.

One particular incident of overwhelm that really showed me how my inner child still needed a lot of support was when I went to a creative arts week in Italy. I was staying at an Ashram in the mountains, just outside Assisi, and each day I went to 'play' at the art academy, which was a short stroll down the road from the Ashram. Everyone was so kind and loving. I had an amazing week on many levels and had given my inner child permission to express herself through the medium of art – it was so healing and liberating. When it came to leave the retreat, I was due to stay a couple of nights in Perugia before my flight left. I had pre-booked a small hotel and duly arrived. It was a bit of a culture shock after having been in such a safe and held space at the Ashram, and the first night of leaving my hotel was a challenge. I had to walk around a strange town on my own with no idea of where I was or where to go. My anxiety started to build, and before I knew it, I was in total overwhelm – it was a combination of things, but one of the biggest triggers for me was the fact that I had to go and eat on my own. I felt like everyone was looking at me thinking, why is she on her own – what a loser! I felt so uncomfortable and tragically sad inside, and once I ate my meal I went back to my hotel room and just wanted to hide away. I felt so vulnerable and alone, and totally out of my depth. I cried myself to sleep, and when I woke the next morning, I just knew I had to turn things around, as I had another whole day and night before my flight home and I really wanted to enjoy the rest of my stay the best I could.

I sat myself down and did what I knew would work. I meditated, did some yoga and spoke lovingly and gently to that little girl within. I reassured her and held her – I told her that I, the adult, was capable and responsible for her, was there for her and would look after her. I soothed her, I adored her, I loved her and I held her hand.

All I can say is that the difference I felt when I left my hotel room this time was immense. It was like a different person walking out into the morning sunlight, and I was back in alignment and seeing through the eyes of Love as a capable, strong and trusting woman. Needless to say, I had a totally different experience and enjoyed a wonderful day exploring the beautiful town, feeling so relaxed, confident and in the flow. I even struck up a couple of conversations with the locals, as I sat in the town square watching the world go by, and it didn't matter that we didn't speak the same language, we were in the moment, alive and just sharing the simple pleasure of connection. It was such a joy for me and I came to learn something profoundly important that day. I came to understand what it meant to be a fully functioning adult and one who trusted herself, and who needn't feel inadequate or inferior any more. Just as importantly, I knew that I could call on this experience again if I felt a similar feeling, and instead of being totally lost, I knew I could shift my energy, comfort my inner child and return to Love.

I now feel so much more confident when I travel abroad and my inner child is extremely happy, adventurous and loves taking me to many magical and exciting places. Furthermore, she is a delight to be with!

I would encourage you to build a relationship with this part of you and get the right help to support you to learn to re-parent your inner child. Don't put up your defences and gleam that your childhood was perfect and that your parents were faultless. This is not about blame at all and, yes, your parents did the best they could with their own set of circumstances. It's about taking self-responsibility for your own happiness and setting yourself, and everyone else, free. Eventually when you pass through this stage you will see that the original wound of your child was the separation from God, but inner child healing is an important part to reach that final destination.

The Young Ones

The young ones now come in with more gusto than previous generations, presenting their uniqueness in a multitude of different ways, commonly struggling to fit in, being hypersensitive or with labels such has autism, dyslexia, ADHD or the 'troubled one'. Whichever way they show up in the world, they are highly intelligent, creative geniuses demanding the true meaning of unconditional love. They are shaking up the world like never before and, as such, we need to honour their brilliance and be able to support them to move through life in their individual way. You may be a parent or caregiver for one of these beautiful souls or you may recognise yourself as one who is in this particular camp.

More and more children are arriving with less tolerance to fitting in and playing by the rules of old, and I say amen to that! They are not willing to fit the mould and will freely express their feelings demanding to be treated as an equal. In many cases parents and teachers recognise that these young souls need to be respected in their own right, and are able to embrace the differences and commit to helping them be in the world as they are, giving them outlets and tools to manage their emotions, creativity and self-expression. Conversely there are still adults, be they parents, teachers or professionals, who think they know best and try to force them to fit into a particular box, medicate them or abuse them mentally or physically. They can't cope with these bright ones being so different and can feel uncomfortable as they witness these dear souls wanting their freedom. Many of us have been taught to make good citizens out of these kids, just so they fit in to the conventional world, but in actual fact, this diminishes their light instead of enhancing it.

I know that the reaction of parents, teachers, etc., is well meaning and that many of us have been conditioned to think that as the adult/parent we know best. But we have to be willing to open our minds, get out of the way and trust that these kids have their own natural guidance system, which is to be nurtured not suppressed. This doesn't mean we aren't there for them or don't support them – no not at all, it means we turn to Love not fear.

It can be really hard to let go and really let Love guide our children, because we want to protect them, guide them from our point of view and, in many cases, wrap them up in cotton wool, but this actually does more harm than good. Each generation needs to grow and expand in its unique way – this is natural and healthy, and not to be resisted.

Do you remember the day when hitting as a form of punishment was mainstream and the defence was "it never did me any harm", "it's for their own good", etc. We can see clearly that this was not the case and has damaged many generations. The shift can't happen overnight, it takes time, but we have to see our own patterns first before we can truly love our kids without conditions. We have to step back and support them to find their way – the new way – the way we are not necessarily going to be part of!

When we come from the heart and not from fear, we can then guide our children from a completely different energy and support them to align with their own hearts too. Let's not feed them with the fear we grew up with, they deserve more than that. Let them be different, let them be true to themselves and be our teachers, and show us the true meaning of Love.

The young ones are leaping in fully awake as long as we allow it. We won't have a clue what is going on because they are light years away. Autism is the way ahead – they are always right – they are sublime in their honesty. They see through all the crap!
Sarah Cox[12]

Chapter 7

The Times They are a Changing

I hope by now that with what I have shared so far, you can see how the SA journey is not black and white, and, ultimately, each one of us will have our own unique experiences. There are not many people who 'wake up' instantly; it takes time, tenderness and a lot of surrender. We are letting go of our old identity and choosing instead to unwind our minds from the egoic world of control. To be free and able to shine our light, we need to be open to doing the inner work, and to understand what is happening as part of our SA.

I, therefore, feel it's important at this point to identify and look at the commonalities of a SA, and in this chapter, I want to highlight the typical signs, symptoms and traits that you may have already gone through, are right in the middle of or are in the process of healing.

Many of the symptoms can be deemed as 'normality' or just one of those things that happen in life. And yes, to a degree, that is the case, or at least in the egoic and conventional world. However, when we are wanting to relinquish the old ways and step into our natural state of being, the generic label of 'normality' can, in fact, hide that you are awakening. The symptoms are just an outpouring of a deep disconnect which are pointing us in the direction of change, but if you are not even aware that you are going through a SA, what the hell are you supposed to do? If you're like most people you may have gone to your GP worried or concerned about certain physical or mental symptoms, but, of course, they don't cover the topic of anything vaguely metaphysical or spiritual, so they're not going to diagnose a SA! They can only follow the conventional path that they have been trained to do and, therefore, put you in one box or another with your diagnoses and off you go into the system. This covering over the 'wound' with a plaster and a 'there, there' is the best they can do, because they too are just lost in the game they were taught to play. This is not meant to belittle or undermine anyone, because I know that everyone is doing the very best they can with their understanding of a 3D world. This awakening process is rarely understood by most people, and that is why I feel so honoured to be sharing this information to help and support the growing need for transparency and spiritual wisdom.

What emerged for me in the early days of my SA were many physical as well as emotional changes. Here are a few examples:

Body: I became very sensitive to certain skin and hair products and I couldn't bear the smell of artificial perfumes, deodorants or air fresheners. On top of that, I found that certain foods I could normally eat became a problem, and alcohol sent me over the edge and I would feel ill, very quickly. I was tired and overwhelmed a lot of the time and pushing myself to keep going.

Friendships and Relationships: I found myself just not fitting in, and feeling totally disconnected to the old way of relating, i.e., gossip, drama, blame or idle chitter-chatter. I was craving deeper connection, but had no idea how to do that and, subsequently, drew back and hid away.

Environment: I became less and less satisfied with 'normal' things like shopping, being in a job, socialising or joining in with the 'injustices' of the world. I craved simplicity, nature and truth.

Energy: I started to pick up on energy and the vibe of people, places or situations. Shopping centres became a no-go area as everything seemed louder, intense and overwhelming. I could also sense when people were insincere, hiding or playing some game, and I had no desire to be in that space. This heightened sensitivity was such a new experience for me. It felt frightening and I thought I was losing the plot, and in a way, I was – the plot of the ego.

I was, of course, completely unaware of what was happening at that stage, but once I did realise and I started to join the dots, it was such a relief to know what was really happening. As time went on and I started to talk to more people, I realised I wasn't alone and that many were also going through similar things. I started to see patterns and themes and eventually knew that this phenomenon was real.

There is no textbook awakening as such, so I thought it would be helpful to provide a list showing some of the changes and ways in which we can support ourselves throughout this process, without freaking out and thinking we are going completely insane. This list shows some, but I am sure not all 'symptoms', so please know that if there is something that is personal to you and it is not listed, it does not mean it is not valid; it just means it has not been listed.

Physical & Emotional Changes

- Sensitivity to different foods, alcohol and skin products
- Heightened emotions
- Unease within certain relationships
- Unable to join others in gossip, anger or blame anymore
- Confusion and uncertainty about what you want or need
- Feeling disorientated, light-headed or dizzy
- Physical ailments seem to get worse or new ones appear
- A sense of injustice and not feeling understood
- Wanting to retreat and hide away
- Feeling like you're invisible and are not truly heard

- Unease in particular environments: work, shops or social venues
- Heightened emotions like anger, which make you feel rageful towards people, places or even yourself
- Feeling like you just don't fit in or talk the same language
- Feeling alone and isolated
- Wanting to kill yourself and escape forever
- Feeling a deep calling within and a knowing that something isn't right and there has to be another way

You may resonate with some or all of these – there is no right or wrong, and know that this is not a measure of how well you are doing, or not. They are pointers and it can be reassuring to know that change is, indeed, happening. I want to reassure you that this is perfectly normal as our bodies and souls begin to realign and recalibrate energetically. For some, this may only be slight, whilst for others it may be a huge biological upgrade, which can feel very frightening and overwhelming.

Bear in mind, that these symptoms are the beginning of the body letting go of what no longer serves and are part of moving on and through, to a more balanced place. The body is incredibly wise and the energy system within knows what it needs to do, so please trust this process and know it will pass, and the more accepting of this you are, the easier it will be.

It reminds me of those times when I supported clients in my Hypnotherapy practice to give up smoking. Inevitably there were many changes within the body, as it got on with the job of removing the crap that had accumulated throughout the years of smoking. More often than not, clients would have cold or flu-like symptoms with torrents of phlegm leaving the body, as well as heightened emotions and insecurities. Some people would also report that their breathing got worse to start with and this could be very disconcerting, as they had expected their breathing would get easier. Lungs hold grief, so not only were clients dealing with breaking free from the addiction and habit, but they were beginning to feel their supressed emotions.

It's perfectly logical to see that when the crutch (smoking) was taken away, the symptoms were exacerbated, but it actually shows that the body's natural ability to heal has kicked in and the immune system now has a chance to do its job of bringing back balance and equilibrium. The billions of cells in our body instinctively know what they need to do – it is a remarkable mechanism, which can heal anything, so we need to honour and trust that it needs time, tenderness and acceptance during this transition.

In the trade, these side effects are known as a Healing Crisis and this is quite literally a biological upgrade, and it's no different with a SA. Things will change as the soul starts to shake off the burdens, masks and shell that the body wore for protection. This process is actually very beautiful, as we learn to truly listen to our body, instead of ignoring its messages. In time we will become consciously aware of the signs that our body is offering us instead of ignoring them, and we will learn to be guided by them. The more willing and present we become to the changes that are manifesting, the more able we are to be there for ourselves instead of running away from our feelings or transferring the blame on to the world outside of us.

Things can get worse before they get better and I know you probably don't want to hear that. But take heart as, just like being a non-smoker, the benefits far outweigh being a smoker. The cleansing of your mind, body and spirit is a healthy part of the SA. As we clear the decks, so we become a clearer channel of energy and thus allow the boundless well-being and Love to enter.

I also want to add at this point that, once you are on the path of a SA, there really isn't any way of turning back. You may want to go back to normality (whatever that is) or pull over for a while and take a rest, I know I did for sure. It is okay to take a rest, so do it and don't beat yourself up. The Universe will go at your pace and in ways that are right for you. There is no hurry at all, but continue it will, because your heart is calling you onwards... If you go with the flow and allow the wave to take you, instead of trying to swim against it – it will be a much smoother ride.

Awakening is a life's work of self-mastery and curiosity. I can see how it would be easier to pop a pill as it is very intense when you are feeling all these new feelings. I did medicate, but my behaviour was even more crazy – I couldn't do it. It doesn't have to be traumatic if you can learn to trust your own inner compass and intuition. Learn to listen to your inner guidance and find what you need to plug you in.
Kat Byles[13]

Supporting Yourself

We have established that stuff is going to happen, things will fall away and life will never quite look the same. This is part of the natural expansion of your soul and we are all part of a much bigger picture than just the material world of matter and form. There is a magnetic force that is drawing us to the Divine Source of Love, just like a compass that is drawn to its natural north pole. We can't stop it – no matter how hard we try; the pull is beyond our control. But what is in our control is the decision to trust its pull and let it show us the way instead of us thinking we know best.

Many have tried to override the pull and use their free will, just as they have been taught, but unfortunately this only leads to a life of littleness, which compared to the magnitude that is awaiting in the new paradigm is just tragic.

I was shown time and time again an image of a jigsaw puzzle, which was a metaphor for the picture of my old life. When the SA hit, the whole jigsaw puzzle was thrown high up into the air and my old identity along with it. Little by little the pieces of the puzzle began to land, forming a brand-new picture orchestrated with exquisite expression from the Universe. Each piece was new, only landing when it was ready to and in the part of the picture that fitted it perfectly. If we rush it or force it, we end up with pieces missing, pieces that are forced to fit and pieces that just look cheap and shabby. That's how the ego wants it to be, but you are worth so much more than that, friends. You are worth the whole enchilada, and so we really do need to be patient and trust that the end result will be worth it!

So please don't be despondent when you go through this stage; know it is perfectly normal and healthy, and a very positive sign of healing and transformation. Remember also, that nothing stays the same and change is inevitable – the butterfly, the flower, the grain of corn, each go through a transformational process to become what they are meant to be. They were once in the darkness and it's the same for you too.

The ego will become a little affronted as you start to change, as it really doesn't like you doing things differently. Ultimately, it's losing its identity and that is an excruciating prospect for it and it will do anything it can to hook you back into the old ways. That's why so many people find it hard to break the habitual hardwired patterns and can feel really overwhelmed by the change that is coming. It is, therefore, crucial to foster new ways of being present and mindful, as well as becoming aware of what we need to support us through the transitional period, and that is why self-care is so important.

Self-Care

Self-care is so much more than just getting dressed, washing our face and eating a meal. It's about listening to what we really need first and foremost, and committing to making this a priority. To me that is called healthy self-love, but for some, this may be seen as selfish and an alien concept, and where the incorrect label of narcissism can be pointed.

We are learning to look after our well-being and crucially filling our own cup up first, because if it's empty or leaking out, we literally have nothing to give. Many people live this way and think that this is a worthy way to be, but trust me, friends, eventually you will be running on empty and the consequences will not be the ride you had in mind – it will be a road of many potholes and eventual breakdown.

When our cup is full we are able to give from a joyous, loving, generous and full heart. There won't be any expectations, IOUs or transference of responsibility for another to be our supply. We take full responsibility, and in so doing, radiate a healthy and balanced aura, and the relationships we attract are clean, honest, authentic and playful.

What does self-care look like?

- Taking time out to do what you love without feeling guilty or having to justify it.
- Expressing your needs and wants in a calm and open way.
- Saying no without a blow-by-blow account of why.
- Saying yes to new adventures, experiences and desires of your heart.
- No people-pleasing (see Chapter 8, page 98 for further details on this subject).
- Walking away from stressful or unloving situations or people.
- Radical honesty.
- Being calm, present and open when sharing, without having to blame another.
- Having time on your own if you need it.
- Sharing time with those you love and respect, when you need to.

- Giving yourself permission to be creative, self-expressive or playful.
- Resting, sleeping and chilling out when you feel the need (guilt free!).
- Looking in the mirror and seeing the inner beauty of your soul and saying, "I love you."
- Finding a spiritual practice that works for you. Yoga, meditation, tai chi, dance, writing, pottery, art, crafting, being in nature, journalling, etc., and committing to making this a regular part of your life.
- Treating your body with kindness: drinking water, eating healthy food, taking long baths or invigorating showers, taking time for conscious touch through massage or caressing of your own skin.
- Refraining from harsh environments.
- Choosing inspiring and soothing pastimes.
- Refraining from reading newspapers, the news, soap operas or violent films.
- Time out from social media.
- Refraining from complaining verbally and internally.
- Making lists of things to appreciate in your life.

I have no doubt that for some of you, self-care/self-love will elicit a lot of resistance – I know it did in me, as I was taught, like many, that we have to put everyone else first and be bottom of the pecking order. But under the surface of this erroneous belief is one of the deepest collective wounds that festers away, and that is guilt. Furthermore, if we continue in this vein for long enough, we either become people-pleasers with an inferior disposition in life, feeling totally unworthy of anything vaguely joyous, or the other extreme, which is volcanic flare-ups/outbursts of uncontrollable anger, bitterness, cynicism and harsh judgements. Either way we energetically push away love and all the good things in life, and basically, it sucks the joy out of us and the ability to live from the heart.

I certainly know my own cup was very empty and the needle on the dial was on high alert by the time I actually started to, tentatively, fill my own cup up. It felt so alien to me and I came to see that I had taken on the belief, like many people, that sacrifice was a worthy cause! It seems crazy now, but it's like we wear a badge of honour, with 'look at me, I am doing all these things for other people, aren't I a good person'! But if you're anything like me, it was done through pursed lips, a lot of sighing and tutting along with a sprinkling of resentment thrown in. All subconscious, of course.

This level of behaviour results in rigidity of body and mind, and the crazy thing is that we really do think this is the normal way to live. We have been hypnotised into believing that this is what love looks like, and even more damaging, is the subconscious collective belief that to suffer is a worthy cause! It's subtle, I'll grant you, but once you start to question your thinking and your egoic personality, you will see the insidious belief unfolding before your very eyes. It takes courage to be willing to see these behaviours, but once we do, it frees up a hell of a lot of stagnant energy.

It can be helpful to see how much self-care and self-love you have allowed up to this point, and see where you can begin to start to fill up your own cup. On a scale of 1 to 10, with 10 being full and 0 empty, where is your dial right now? Trust the first number that comes to your mind and don't try and override it, analyse it or paint a rosy picture, just trust what comes up. Wherever it is, please don't feel guilty or ashamed. Just use it as a measure to show you that it is time to change, and be committed to receiving and opening up to a new way of personal self-care and acceptance, aiming to have a cup that is overflowing.

Now you have noticed how full your cup is, how are you feeling – I mean really feeling? Just sit in stillness and take a couple of breaths, relax your body and notice the now moment.

Then ask yourself, how would it be to have a full cup? Just sit with that thought for a moment. Notice what comes up for you... maybe it's euphoria and a big 'yes please, let's do this', maybe it's guilt, a sense of not being worthy of a full cup or fear over what other people will think. Write down whatever comes up for you and just let it have a voice.

Once this has been given its expression, just come back to your breath again, and ask yourself what could you do to move one notch up the scale – what would that look like, feel like or sound like? Take ownership of your ability to let more in and to receiving all the good you deserve. Then affirm, "It's okay to want good things and to take care of myself in a gentle and loving way. The Universe/God wants to give me the best of everything. As I trust in this ever-giving benevolent force, it fills my life with an abundance of love, well-being, joy, peace and serenity. And so it is – thank you, thank you, thank you."

Just let this settle into your being and trust that your life will start to open and you will naturally now want to fill your cup up. It can be helpful to make a list of the things that would support you to do this and, if you find this difficult, maybe take a leaf out of someone else's book and think about what others do to look after themselves in this way. Maybe this will inspire you to try it too.

Managing To Stay True To Yourself

As you start to get clear about self-care and look after yourself, others around you may kick off, because people don't like change, they want things to stay the same. They may come up with all kinds of ways to belittle you or get you to return to the 'old you'. This may be subtle or manipulative, but remember, don't join them in the battle as they are just lost in their own fear. As A Course in Miracles says – if there is any attack or defence, it is a cry for Love, so practise being defenceless (your ego will hate this), but be mindful of keeping true to your heart and listening to your inner guidance.

Refrain, if you can, from justifying your changes; instead just hear the other person and acknowledge their concerns in a loving and meaningful way. Quite often, just by saying to them, "I hear you," a softening will ensue. You are not agreeing or disagreeing, simply honouring their opinion. If you feel guided to, you can just open up and say that you are changing your behaviours and finding new ways of connecting with people that are more authentic and loving. Admit to them that this is new for you and you are just finding your way, and that you hope they understand and can support you through these changing times. Little by little if you keep in this loving place, people usually become more accepting.

Continue to be as honest and authentic as you can, and be brave enough to always speak from your heart and from the 'I' perspective. Remember not to have this kind of encounter when you are feeling overwhelmed, angry or in trauma, as you will be coming from the ego – take time to nurture yourself and settle back into a place of openness and presence. Once you are in that place, then share your innermost feelings if it feels appropriate, and don't expect anything back unless you have specifically asked for feedback, suggestions or a hug. If the other person can't freely give this, trust that it's not personal, it's just that they can't give it now and they don't need to explain or justify it if they do not wish to.

What I have found is that some people who can't deal with the new you may fall away, whilst those who are accepting of your changes will be less critical. You are both finding a new way of relating and it can feel awkward and clunky like any new pattern that is learnt. Think of the first time you got behind the wheel of a car – it felt overwhelming and somewhat daunting, but bit by bit, you mastered the controls, learnt to trust yourself and came to enjoy the thrill of being on the open road and the freedom that it gave you.

It takes practice, and little by little you will spot your own way of people-pleasing and will also learn to recognise how heavy it feels to carry other people's burdens. You don't have to take them on; let's face it, you've had enough of your own to carry and it serves no one. Soon you will find ways to honour yourself, as well as another, and the energy will shift. Just be as present as you can and don't give yourself a hard time if you have a wobble. It's how we learn and you should be incredibly proud that you are trusting this process and making such phenomenal changes in your life and relationships. So please be gentle with yourself and don't beat yourself up if you don't 'get it right' immediately – ditch the perfectionism and self-annihilation, and just trust that you are in a process of healing. Love can handle it all and Love is right there for you helping you to find a place of stillness and acceptance. Remember it's okay to reach out for help from a professional, spiritual mentor or therapist who can support you through this process. It's important to have someone who is not emotionally involved and can hold a space of love whilst keeping the vision of your wholeness.

My wife was so angry with me, as was my business partner because I started to stand up for myself and say no. Many of my friends also thought I had been brainwashed and I said yes I have, my brain needed washing!
John Campbell[14]

Chapter 8

Taking Self-Responsibility

Taking responsibility for our physical, mental and emotional well-being walks hand in hand with our spiritual awakening. One area that came up a lot for me and for those I now work with is dismantling and uprooting the old hand-me-down beliefs and inner voice of the ego. The ego has perfected some pretty brutal scripts and I saw how these scripts ran the show for much of my life. In most cases they were just patterns from previous generations. Some were blatantly harsh jibes loaded with guilt, whilst others were kind of well-meaning, but equally damaging. You may recognise some:

- *Who do you think you are?*
- *Don't get too big for your boots*
- *Don't rock the boat*
- *Children should be seen and not heard*
- *I'm your parent and I know best*
- *I'm in charge and you should do as I say*
- *How dare you*
- *It's a dog-eat-dog world out there*
- *Watch your back*
- *It never did me any harm*
- *No pain no gain*
- *Big boys don't cry*
- *Man up*
- *Good girls don't get angry*
- *I want doesn't get*
- *Aaaah poor you*
- *Do anything for a quiet life*

And so these character assassinations put us firmly in our place, and just as we know that hitting, bullying or coercing a child, or an adult for that matter, is abusive, unhealthy and not at all conducive to a loving and respectful relationship, we need to see that our words are just as damaging and poisonous, leaving deep inner scars.

This childhood programming can manifest in variable levels of self-loathing, self-hate, low self-esteem, shame and fear. It's like being one of the walking dead, until we can get conscious enough to see what is really going on. You can be one of the lucky ones, if you choose, and take responsibility for uncovering these false premises. Understandably, you may find yourself getting angry or upset as you recognise these beliefs. You may also find yourself trying to justify or defend whoever it was that told you these lies. This, as we are discovering, is the ego's natural default setting to either attack or defend its supremacy.

I invite you to take a moment to notice what commentary is running right now within you about this subject and make a list of some of the old belief systems that you were taught as you were growing up and, as you do, you may start to correlate your current behaviours with the conditioning you have taken on. For example, if you were told to 'man up' and not cry as a child, you may find that as an adult you can't express your feelings, and either have a very short fuse and get angry quickly or suppress your needs, thus compromising your truth. The knock-on effect may be that when you are face to face with a difficult situation or a much-needed conversation to resolve an issue, you either metaphorically run away, deflect your feelings or bury yourself in an addiction. The old programme from your childhood renders you unable to face the situation just in case there is the possibility that it may trigger tears of sorrow, upset or pain – I mean what would 'people' think!

One of the biggies for me was "don't get too big for your boots". Basically, this belief trained me to hide, play small, feel less than and keep my own desires and dreams to a minimum. The truth is, that we are meant to shine, we are meant to be all that we are, and apologies or self-put-downs are the opposite of Love, they are the ego's assassination manifesto.

Once we start to expose these beliefs and bring them out from the darkness and into the light, there is then an opportunity for true transparency and healing. The old emotions that may have been locked away now have the chance to be witnessed and expressed with true empathy and loving kindness. This awareness is a crucial part of our SA, and to be free, we have to be able to, not only, forgive our past, and that includes those who 'abused' us knowingly or unknowingly, but also forgive ourselves for actually separating from our Source in the first place.

Once we unveil the old ways and self-sabotage talk we can then practise turning them around – you may find these turnarounds listed below helpful, but also feel free to replace them with affirming statements that speak to you. As soon as you spot the old ego story coming up, stop and then repeat several times the new loving statement to yourself as often as you can. This helps not only to reprogramme the mind, but also reaffirms more loving and truthful statements, which, with practice, will dilute the power they hold over you. It can be very helpful to print some small slips of paper, with the new statement written on them, and then put them in different places that will help prompt you to affirm the new. For example, put them in your purse/wallet, on your bathroom mirror, on the dashboard of your car, on the fridge, inside your coat pocket or next to your workstation. Get inventive and allow your inspiration to conjure up statements that feel loving, affirming and kind to you.

Who do you think you are?	*I am a child of God*
Don't get too big for your boots	*I am the light of the world*
Don't rock the boat	*I am free to express my own opinions*

Children should be seen and not heard	I am entitled to speak my truth
I'm your parent and I know best	I have an inner guidance system that is true for me and guides me well
I'm in charge and you should do as I say	I trust I can listen to my own heart
How dare you	I celebrate who I am
It's a dog-eat-dog world out there	I am sustained by the Love of God
Watch your back	I am safe and held eternally
It never did me any harm	I am dedicated to kindness and self-care – I'm worth it
No pain no gain	I will not hurt myself or another and take my time to make decisions that are guided by love
Big boys don't cry	Feelings and emotions are natural and healthy, and to be expressed and honoured
Man up	It's okay to be vulnerable – I am innocent
Good girls don't get angry	I appreciate being able to express myself in a healthy way
I want doesn't get	The Universe is limitless and I am a child of the Universe
Aaaah poor you	I am spirit, whole and complete
Do anything for a quiet life	It's perfectly okay to say no and respect my own needs without apology or justification

In my defencelessness my safety lies.
A Course in Miracles[15]

It takes balls to put our head above the parapet and be the one to shake things up. I'm not going to say that this stage is an easy one. It can seem a very lonely place for a while, as we sift and sort what is true for us, but ultimately we are responsible for our own behaviour, and as we learn to put ourselves first, we start to become healthy, emotionally-balanced people, knowing our boundaries, able to express our feelings, speak our truth and trust in the wisdom of our heart. The great news is that as we look after ourselves and align with Love, we naturally have so much more to give and actually have an excess to share.

When we choose to support or help another, it now comes from a place of authenticity and a full heart that just wants to give, and give without expecting anything in return. This is the true meaning of unconditional Love – in other words, I don't give to get, I give because it feels good to give regardless of your response or feedback – I give because it is true for me and feels natural and loving. In short, I don't need you for my happiness and you don't need me for your happiness – happiness is an inside job!! When we come together we show up as ourselves, warts and all, and can be honest and real. This, my friends, is true intimacy.

This emotional and spiritual intelligence is so powerful, and the environment is free from mind games, uncertainty or confusion, and the language we use is clear, uncluttered and without a need to be esteemed. For those of us who do not have this model in our lives, we need to be willing to heal the old ways, and take responsibility for our own self-worth and turn around the misconception that someone outside of us can esteem us. We turn instead to our own one true supply – which is infinite, boundless and ever giving, and as we sustain this relationship and make it our daily plug-in we can fill up our own cup.

Gandhi said that, *"We are the change we wish to see in the world,"* and this is how we do it, one day at a time. We wake up each new beautiful day, rub our sleepy eyes and see a whole new world emerging. The ripple effect is monumental, and we are not doing this for recognition or polishing our halo. We must come from a place of non-attachment to the outcome. We are doing it because, first and foremost, we feel better and in alignment with our true Source of Love and happiness! And in my experience being around people who are in alignment, open-hearted and true to themselves is a wonderful place to be.

Meditation and Prayer

To build on this and find ways to maintain alignment and open our hearts, I believe that we must turn to practising two of the key spiritual pathways, which are meditation and prayer.

They are tools to enable you to slow down, become present and open up your vital energy field, which is within you and all around you. Most people don't even realise that they are energetic beings, and have the capability of tuning into this energy field and harnessing it for their well-being and sustenance. Once you do, you will never want to be apart from it or look to others for your guidance, because your natural inherent satnav is 100% accurate and totally on your side.

Meditation

Meditation is about slowing down, becoming present and opening up to the now. The now is potent, full of potential and the only place where you will connect with the Divine Source and its loving guidance. Meditation has also been shown to soothe the soul, as well as measurably change the stress levels of the body, which in turn boosts the immune system. Basically, it's a win-win, and I can guarantee that if you make this a regular practice you will be a much happier person to be around too!

I was a complete novice when I came across meditation as part of my Holistic Therapies Diploma Course back in 1999. We were expected to partake in the weekly meditation class and I can honestly say I was as green as they come. I was also totally sceptical and a little scared too, and just couldn't understand what all the fuss was about. I remember the first time I had to sit down and meditate, I felt nothing at all and halfway through I opened half an eye to see what everyone else was doing. Most people looked peaceful and some even looked like they were in an altered state, and once the meditation was finished would report all kinds of insights, visions and breakthroughs. I, however, was feeling so darn ambivalent and ever so slightly embarrassed about the whole thing and just wanted to get the hell out of there. But, each week I dutifully turned up and would will something to happen – what I was expecting to happen, I really had no concept of back then, as I was still in the world of performance and perfectionism and wanted to 'get it right'. Eventually I got to the point where I thought to myself, well I'm not gonna get this, so why not just enjoy the rest and have some time out. This was quite an appealing thought at the time, as my life outside of college was full on, and time to do nothing was rare. So, I thought, what the heck – let's just chill, and I forgot about meditating altogether and enjoyed this time to relax.

Well, you guessed it, as soon as I stopped trying, something happened! I began to experience different things and saw images, shapes and colours, as well as having minuscule moments of inner stillness. I didn't really know what it all meant, but I was beginning to be okay with the whole idea of meditation. I'm not going to say that I became an avid meditator at that point, because I didn't, but it planted a seed of possibility, that would later germinate into something that I came to love. So never say never, and if I can do it, then so can YOU – yes, YOU!

There are many forms of meditation, and if you are completely new, I would encourage you to find a group if you can. It is so helpful to be able to connect with others, and I know for myself, that I learnt so much just from listening to other people's experiences, as well as being held in a safe space, where I could just let go and get out of the way. There are also hundreds of amazing recordings online, various apps to download along with CDs and YouTube clips.

Ask to be guided to the right thing for you and be open to the Universe delivering what you need. Don't be too hard on yourself if you don't have the most sublime meditation experience or soar to the heights of heaven right away; you're doing just fine. Simply keep open and receptive, and know it takes time and practice.

Equally if you are experienced in meditation, know that the more you deepen into your practice the more you will open up to mystical and illuminating experiences.

Meditation traditionally is done sitting down, but can also become an everyday part of your life incorporating mindfulness and presence, whilst partaking in any activity. Walking, cooking, cleaning or shopping can be meditation in movement. It's about giving 100% attention to the moment regardless of what you are doing as well as having a curious childlike innocence… I can't emphasise this innocence enough, because it means we see through eyes of wonder and awe every new day, instead of dragging around our past and jaded ego.

Imagine, for a moment, that you got a bang on the head and lost your short-term memory, and each morning when you awaken you have no recollection of the previous day or anybody in your life – absolutely nothing! Take a moment just to feel how that would be for you. It would mean that you would not bring any old judgements, grievances, expectations, hurts, jealousy, envy or attachments from the past. Then consider as you went about your new day how you would look at everyone and everything totally afresh. Wow – just imagine!!!!

This is truly looking through the eyes of Love and being totally in the now. That is what your life can be like every day, if you so choose. For some inspiration do check out the movie *50 First Dates* starring Drew Barrymore and Adam Sandler. It's a real eye-opener as well as a touching and funny movie that portrays exactly this scenario.

Prayer

Prayer is not a 'spare wheel' that you pull out when in trouble, but it's a 'steering wheel' that directs the right path all of life.
Unknown

Prayer is something that I thought was only for religious people and so I baulked at the idea of it – I mean, who the hell was I praying to! But I came to understand that prayer was building a relationship to a power greater than myself, and like any relationship we need to practise honest communication, vulnerability and willingness. We have to drop our guard and let someone in, and it's no different with prayer. We are opening up to the Divine and it wants to communicate with us too, but we have to meet it halfway and prayer is that meeting point.

So just start, start anywhere. Just start to have a conversation in your head, a chat, an open dialogue and ask for help. Be humble enough to know that you can't live this life on your own, and you don't need to. Admit that you don't know, admit that you have screwed it up, admit that you want help and admit that something amazing will happen. And don't just pray when you're in trouble; that can feel like pleading and smacks of victimhood. Don't get me wrong, I've been there – I have pleaded in total desperation and there is nothing to feel guilty about, but what I'm encouraging you to do is to get to the point where it is natural to ask and converse with your Higher Power through prayer. You will soon start to see the repercussions and miracles on a daily basis.

Make the prayers up or start to use some that others have used – nobody cares! There are many out there and you will start to find what fits for you, and before you know it, it will become natural and an integral part of your life. Always remember to acknowledge the insights, guidance and aha moments that transpire – say thank you, because this builds the muscle of trust and deepens your personal relationships to the God of your understanding.

Here are a few examples you may find helpful, and remember to use the word that fits for you and, if need be, take God out of the equation and replace it with what feels true for you. The ego will find every trick in the book to stop you connecting with your Source, so be vigilant of the excuses and so-called legitimate reasons why not to pray or meditate, but just do it anyway – let's face it, what have you got to lose?

Dear God
May Your JOY be my angel today
May Your JOY be my music today
May Your JOY be my teacher today
May Your JOY be my healer today
May Your JOY be my purpose today
Amen
Robert Holden[16]

The Serenity Prayer
God grant me the serenity to accept the things I cannot change, courage to change the things I can; and wisdom to know the difference. Amen.
Reinhold Niebuhr

I am here only to be truly helpful. I am here to represent Him Who sent me. I do not have to worry about what to say or what to do, because He Who sent me will direct me. I am content to be wherever He wishes, knowing He goes there with me. I will be healed as I let Him teach me to heal.
A Course in Miracles[17]

Dear God, please help me to recognise the truth about myself, no matter how beautiful it is.
Alan Cohen

In the infinity of life where I am, all is whole, perfect and complete. I am one with the Power that created me. I am totally open and receptive to the abundant flow of prosperity that the Universe offers. All my needs and desires are met before I even ask. I am Divinely guided and protected, and I make choices that are beneficial for me. I rejoice in others' successes, knowing there is plenty for all. I am constantly increasing my conscious awareness of abundance, and this reflects in a constantly increasing income. My good comes from everywhere and everyone. All is well in my world.

Louise Hay[18]

Deep peace of the running wave to you
Deep peace of the flowing air to you
Deep peace of the quiet earth to you
Deep peace of the shining stars to you
Deep peace of the infinite peace to you
Gaelic Blessing, Unknown

Dear God
I've tried it my way
Now it's over to you
Show me the truth
I am ready and I am willing
I surrender and I come to you with empty hands and an open heart
Thank you
A prayer from yours truly, Ann-Marie

Eventually, with enough commitment you will start to build a daily spiritual practice that incorporates self-care, meditation and prayer, and this, my friend, will stand you in very good stead. It becomes as normal as brushing your teeth, and before you know it, you will be feeling so much more happiness, peace and joy. It's an absolute no brainer for me and my daily plug-in is now completely normal and something that I am not prepared to compromise on, and I bet if you asked anyone who knows me well, they would tell you that I'm a much nicer person to be around these days because of it!

Chapter 9

The Know It All Mind

The next phase I want to talk about was quite a shocker for me. I had come a long way and changed significantly, and thought I had pretty much arrived. Quite where I thought I had arrived to, I had no real concept of, but hey, that's the ego for you! I had indeed read many books of depth and insight, attended courses, been on retreats, had the qualifications and certainly had a good understanding of all things spiritual. But, unfortunately, with this 'I know mind' the ego had created yet another persona – 'The Spiritual/Enlightened One'. Oh boy, it's so sneaky, and if we're not careful, it will keep us stuck here for an eternity!

The way in which I first saw this starting to unfold was with my identity as a therapist. I felt 'qualified' to heal others, and to be fair I certainly was able to help and support people in many ways, but what I didn't appreciate during that phase was that the way in which I thought I was helping people was, in fact, a distraction from my own wounded self.

I was so full of passion to share what I knew and had learnt, and as such, felt an overwhelming urge to preach to the world. In many cases as soon as I met anyone who had a perceived 'problem', I was right on them! You need such and such, you should do this, you should change this, you must take this, do you know about... blah blah blah. I would also vomit spiritual quotes and 'enlightened' answers to all and sundry, whether they wanted to hear it or not! It was well meaning I can assure you, but slightly misguided, and my God, when I think about it now, I really was on a mission to save, what I perceived as, a broken world. I now understand that the broken world I saw was just my inner unhealed mind reflecting my pain outwards, which resulted in my need to micromanage everything.

Right here and now, I apologise profusely to any of you reading this whom I inadvertently vomited over! It was meant with the best will in the world, and if you're still in my life, well done, and thank you for being so understanding!!

I wanted to share what I had learnt with so many people and this pissed off many people at this time but this helped me sort out the people who really understood me and those who didn't resonate anymore. I had to go through that stage as part of my journey – I can see how it was Spiritual Arrogance!
John Campbell[19]

At that particular point of my journey, I came to eventually understand that I had been trying to fill the inner God gap (the space that can only be filled by God) with something or someone outside of myself.

For me this manifested as:

a) being blind and in denial of my own wounds
b) using relationships or another as a distraction
c) assuming that everyone else needed to be fixed and was incapable of working things out for themselves or indeed had a higher power to guide them
d) feeling superior because I was 'qualified' to know what was best for them!

Thankfully, I came to see this blind spot and understood that this urge was, in fact, a form of addiction known as codependency and a deep cry for love. I started to understand that my overbearing need to fix everyone and be in control of everything was coming from a place of deep fear. I was lovingly encouraged by my spiritual mentor to take a look at a way of understanding this pattern and was led to a path of recovery on one of the 12-step programmes. You see there are many forms of addiction (all of which are trying to fill the God gap) not just the obvious ones of alcohol, drugs, shopping and sex, but the subtler ones such as spiritual addiction, destination addiction, busyness and, as mentioned, codependency. I would recommend looking into this if it resonates with you, because in my experience, most relationships have elements of codependency at their core. I personally found it very helpful over a period of about three years to attend a 12-step programme and start to look at my codependency behaviour.

It was hard going to start with, as the light began to illuminate the ways I had been acting out by controlling, blaming, fixing and basically projecting all my stuff on to other people. This initially brought up a lot of guilt and shame, which I found difficult to own. Shame can really dig the knife in to an already wounded lost soul if we let it, but as I came to discover, shame is just another ego projection and one that can bubble up to the surface when we do this deep inner work. It needs a release, because shame is so toxic to the whole system and eats away at the core of our being. You may be familiar with some of the damning shame statements that seem to easily slip off the untrained tongue: 'shame on you/me' and 'you/they should be ashamed of themselves'. Never, never buy into this, my friend, and never, never project it on to others, even if you feel it is justified – it never is!! It actually makes us superior and judgemental, as we decide to point the finger on another in this way – I would suggest you bring the finger back to yourself and see that, yet again, it is another projection of your own inner pain that feels the need to condemn in this way. The ego will come up with many clever defences to deny this; but trust me, if we spot it, we've got it. We have to really check in with ourselves and notice when we are being the judge and jury, and open up to healing this attack thinking and be willing to only look through the eyes of Love and compassion.

The thing we really need to watch is authenticity – I am aware people who are in addiction can go into spiritual addiction and give their power away to gurus, etc., and just because someone has written a book, doesn't mean they know what you need. We need to be surrounded by people who will call us into accountability and say it as it is. We need friends like that, even at the loss of the relationship.
Sarah Cox[20]

I wanted to change, and even though I had a lot of resistance to being part of a 12-step programme (the ego's arrogance didn't feel I was in the same league as others who were deemed as addicts!), I was willing to put the work in. As a result, I soon started to find a way to identify my own needs and a new way of communicating what they were. The focus was on me and my Higher Power which meant that as I learnt to self-love and self-soothe, I was less desperate to transfer my own pain on to everyone else.

I discovered that if someone asks us for our support, we have a choice in how we do that. We first and foremost connect with our own inner guidance and ask how we can be truly helpful – we then wait and see what guidance we are given. Only then do we take action if we feel to do so and also acknowledge that it's okay not to help if it doesn't feel right. We then have to get our hands off what they decide to do, and our only job is to be transparent, authentic, unattached and, of course, Love them regardless of what they decide to do.

Equally, if we feel someone is trying to fix us or tell us what to do and we have not asked for their help or counsel, and we feel bullied to do x, y or z, it is important to be as honest as we can and be okay with saying thanks, but no thanks. It takes courage to do this, but that is part of what the SA journey is about – being true to ourselves and being authentic in our relationships, without fear of rejection, and trusting that the relationship can handle it. We become ready to drop all people-pleasing and, in my experience, once we master this we really are in a much happier place and have found the key to healthy communication.

People-pleasing is what we have been taught to do by others and it can be very subtle to the untrained mind, but once we remove this veil of control it becomes glaringly obvious how it plays out.

People-Pleasing Traits

- You often feel like a doormat and put others' needs before your own
- You worry about hurting others' feelings and letting them down
- You take responsibility for making everyone around you happy
- You believe you are less than others
- You avoid giving yourself credit for anything
- You easily attract people who need to be rescued or consoled
- You apologise for everything
- You rarely ask for or accept help
- You hate confrontation and avoid conflict
- You need praise and acknowledgment to feel good
- You're nice and helpful to everyone you meet, including people you dislike
- You can always be counted on for a favour and then act like a martyr
- You change your tone and behaviours depending on who is around you
- You worry that people won't like you
- You judge yourself harshly
- You can't say no, and if you do you have to explain and justify why
- You feel overwhelmed and burdened a lot of the time

It's quite a comprehensive list, and when I started to take this on board there was a lot of confusion on how to behave, because I thought this people-pleasing behaviour was normal. I had a lot of resistance to change, but little by little with practice and commitment, I began to learn a new way of relating with people. It involved a lot of uncertainty to start with, as I wasn't sure what the response of others would be, because I had been accustomed to walking on eggshells and not upsetting people; but as I became braver and bolder, I shifted my old limiting behaviours and my life became a lot easier and authentic.

During this process I also learnt about boundaries, what they were, what they meant and, more importantly, how to set them in a healthy way. I realised I could say no without having to explain or justify why, and that my no could be guilt free. This was a biggie for me, and the first time I did this in a relationship, I physically felt sick and had to run away to the bathroom and take stock of what I had just done. It was such a new thing to express myself in this way, but miraculously when I came back down to sit with my boyfriend, he was absolutely fine and had no problem with what I had shared. It was only me that felt the discomfort, because I was changing the deep-rooted habits of a lifetime and finding my true voice.

I equally became friends with saying a wholehearted yes to new things, to life and to myself. It felt amazing and I began to understand the freedom that came with this radical honesty. It was like learning a whole new language, but I was feeling the shift and amazed at how much better I felt in my day-to-day life. It was a revelation that I could behave so differently, and I became less reactive and less prone to knee-jerk reactions. Instead I was learning to become still, go within and await my Higher Power's guidance. As a result, I became less affected by other people's insecurities, projections and problems, and trusted that they had their own Higher Power who would guide them. I could, of course, be there for them in the presence of

Love and support them, if it felt appropriate, and if, indeed, they asked for it.

I was now getting the answers to my questions, which I'd asked when my marriage failed. I had wanted to understand what a healthy relationship was, as well as the meaning of true Love. It helped me to see that there was no one to blame and that we had just been acting out our stories and ego attachments in what we called a marriage, and the preconceived false ideas of what a marriage is. It was a relief to see the bigger picture, but also startling, when I saw the construct of a 'special relationship'.

A Special Relationship is a term used in A Course in Miracles, meaning any relationship that we use as a substitute for Oneness with God and unknowingly make an idol of. It can be a special hate relationship, in which we feel justified in projecting hate or anger on to another, or it may be a special 'exclusive' love relationship, where we believe that only one special person can meet our needs and be our everything.

Every special relationship you have made has, as its fundamental purpose, the aim of occupying your mind so completely that you will not hear the call of truth.
A Course in Miracles[21]

It left me with a lot of questions, especially as all I had seen in the world was 'special relationships' and I was hungry to understand what true Love really was. I wanted the Universe to show me examples of this, because to that point, I hadn't come across any, and to be fair how could I, because my radar had only been aligned to the ego's perspective of love.

For most of us, our parents' relationship was our main example of 'love' in our formative years. We may have just had one parent as our role model, if one had died or been absent for some reason. We may also have been adopted, brought up by a foster family, or any other combination. There is no 'normal' family or upbringing, but whatever the circumstances, it was rare to have a fully functioning, totally connected and unconditionally loving example, and on top of that, not many of us were brought up to be able to share our emotions, feelings and inner needs in a healthy way.

If you were one of the lucky ones who were brought up by those who saw the truth and the light in you, then I say celebrate that and be grateful that you had such pure caregivers as an example – but this is rare. Whichever is the case, know that you were born into the perfect family and your soul chose exactly what it needed to learn in this lifetime, and it may be comforting for you to know that the script was already written, so blaming anyone is fruitless and indeed keeps you stuck in pain and suffering.

The Attraction Factor in Intimate Relationships

Once I had delved into my family of origins* (see footnote) and old belief systems, I also came to discover why we attract certain character types in our intimate relationships. This really was a turning point for me and exactly what I needed to shift my old construct of what I thought relationships were about.

*Family of origins: The people who raise us and who we spend most of our childhood with, who pass down old beliefs and behaviours from previous generations.

All relationships are an opportunity for healing and, ultimately, that is why we are in them, whether we realise it or not. Relationships are, of course, a combination of companionship, friendship, joy, sex, laughter and union, but from a spiritual perspective they are two souls coming together to recognise the light and truth within each other, and as such have no hold or attachment to the outcome of the relationship. It is based on freedom, presence, no private thoughts and the Love is not 'special' or 'exclusive' like most people think. It's the capital L Love not the ego small love.

What happens when we are 'asleep' is that we energetically attract another person providing opportunities for exactly what we need to learn. Our soul calls forth another who can help us recognise our own wounds and separation from God, so as to illuminate and then heal them – and vice versa. What I also discovered is that on a deeper level we also tend to attract a partner who is indicative of the parent whom we revered or demonised. This partner will have similar qualities, wounds and traits as one of our parents and, if we are not awake enough to see, this will just continue to play out the role within the relationship.

I was so shocked when I saw this for myself, but it certainly was the case – I had attracted elements of my mother, whom I revered. She adored me and always called me the apple of her eye, she wrapped me up in cotton wool and 'smothered' me with love. I knew nothing else, of course, and adored and loved my mother too, she was my everything. But in her own codependency and lack of self-love, she had used me as her escape from her own deep pain, and in my father, she had attracted the 'demon', and subconsciously I had done the same. I just want to emphasise that the word demon is not used here to imply that someone is the devil or bad, as neither my father nor my husband were either of these. But it is more about the 'role' that is played out in the ego's script, which is only concerned with getting its needs met, which subconsciously only causes separation not true joining.

My husband adored me, put me on a pedestal, and 'needed' me and my love. To start with this felt so wonderful and so heady, and naturally what I thought love was – but little by little, as I realised I could never be his everything or indeed make him happy, I started to resent him and felt totally smothered. And he too was just playing out his own wounded child and had attracted the 'perfect fit' in me, and so it goes on.

It was such a relief to understand what had really happened within my marriage and to gain perspective of the bigger picture. It was mind-blowing, as I saw how much ego fear had been present and how, over time, I had closed my heart to the Big Love, because I had felt so smothered by the ego's small insidious 'love'.

I had so much healing, forgiveness and grieving to do, which was partly looking at my family of origin, as well as undoing the old stories and guilt around intimacy and the ability to speak from my heart. It was tough, but also so revealing, and the honesty that developed over that period of time made for such deeper and sweeter relationships all round. It was so incredibly freeing, and I came to see my parents, my ex-husband and his family through different eyes – I saw the truth and I blessed them all.

The great gift that comes from this profound work is that we clear the slate of our family lineage and in turn clear it for future generations. We can then be totally present in all our relationships and shine as we are meant to, and encourage our loved ones to do the same. It doesn't mean that we have it all figured out, but it does mean we can step back and ask God to help us when we lose our way and let go of thinking we know it all and make forgiveness our priority.

The deepest pain I ever felt was denying my own feelings to make everyone else comfortable.
Nicole Lyons[22]

Learning When To Step Back

I would like to give you an example of when I discovered that I was continuing the old programme of smothering, and how I was able to step back and let God take over.

My daughter was diagnosed with type one diabetes when

she was nine years old, and it was an incredibly distressing time for the whole family. Her words to me as we left the doctor's surgery to go to the hospital, were, "Mummy, am I going to die?" As you can imagine, this triggered a lot of stuff within me, and my protective mummy stepped in big time and just got on with the job of getting her to a hospital and then the very steep learning curve that ensued with this diagnosis.

As a mother I was devastated and overwhelmed and felt such responsibility for the situation. I wanted to 'get it right', keep her safe, support her and make sure she was well looked after. Quite natural, for sure, but under the surface the smothering that I had received as a child was now playing out in this relationship too. This was compounded by my insecurities and fear of my daughter becoming really unwell or dying. I lived in fear on a daily basis – fear of hypos, fear of high blood sugars, fear of what to feed her, fear when she didn't want to inject her insulin, fear of how other people would treat her, fear of her long-term health, fear, fear, fear, and I saw her as a victim of this disease.

Along with the fear and overwhelm, I felt a huge responsibility for every part of her life and didn't trust her to cope without my help. This became unhealthy, particularly when she came to her mid-teens and needed to start spreading her wings, and step out into the world and discover her own life.

Eventually I realised how my 'knowing best', along with a bucketload of guilt, was, in fact, detrimental to her own growth as a young adult. I had to step back and little by little trust her to make her own decisions and start to learn to take responsibility for her own well-being and, of course, build a relationship with her own intuition and ability to tune into her guidance – not mine!

As I did this, there was afterburn as she had become accustomed to mum being in charge for so many years and making all the decisions for her. But gradually as I encouraged her to trust herself and reassured her that she could do it – she began to fly. She started to walk her own path and, in turn, build her confidence muscle for life. Many times, I so wanted to take over, and would have overwhelming urges to step in and stop her from 'making mistakes'! I now know that there are no mistakes to make, only learning opportunities.

I can find only three kinds of business in the universe: mine, yours, and God's. (For me, the word God means 'reality'. Reality is God, because it rules. Anything that's out of my control, your control, and everyone else's control – I call that God's business.)
Byron Katie[23]

I have come to learn that the most loving and supportive thing we can do is to inspire and encourage our children to listen to their own hearts and trust their own inner guidance. If we can teach them this, they will be on a path of true self-esteem, trust and confidence. We must be prepared to put our own desire to 'teach' them what we know on hold and let them build their own God muscle. This does not mean we abandon them. It means we love and encourage them wholeheartedly and envision them as God sees them, whole, loving, abundant, wise, beautiful, all-knowing, vital, vibrant and in alignment. If they stumble or fall, we soothe them and wrap our arms around them with deep love and presence. If they ask us for our advice or how we feel about something, then and only then do we offer our views and possible suggestions. We need to be mindful of the ego's desire to hoodwink the party and come in with all its doom and gloom tales of woe. I now take time to breathe, pray and ask to be truly helpful and ask for the right words to be spoken through me, not of me. It's amazing when we take the time to do this, and results in less drama and pain all round.

The words of Kahlil Gibran are a beautiful reminder here:

On Children[24]

Your children are not your children.
They are the sons and daughters of Life's longing for itself.
They come through you but not from you,
And though they are with you yet they belong not to you.

You may give them your love but not your thoughts,
For they have their own thoughts.
You may house their bodies but not their souls,
For their souls dwell in the house of tomorrow,
Which you cannot visit, not even in your dreams.

You may strive to be like them
But seek not to make them like you.
For life goes not backward nor tarries with yesterday.

You are the bows from which your children as living arrows
are sent forth.
The archer sees the mark upon the path of the infinite and He
bends you with His might
That His arrows may go swift and far.
Let your bending in the archer's hand be for gladness;
For even as He loves the arrow that flies, so He loves also the
bow that is stable.

I encourage you to read this several times with an open heart, and be willing to let it land. I know it is one of the hardest things to take on board as a parent or grandparent, but we have to be willing to let our children go, and to stop interfering with our ideas of what we think is best. Love them with every fibre of your being and bless yourself for being a parent who is healthy, aligned, truthful, transparent and, of course, you will mess it up sometimes. But you will also be someone who will be compassionate to yourself and refuse to play the blame game, and to honour that you are doing your very best, and remember that the 'perfect' parent does not exist. We are all perfectly imperfect – what a relief that is!

Reaping the Rewards and Time To Move On

As a result of my own changes over that period of time, I started to attract relationships that were clean and clear and without drama. I was delighted to be enjoying this new way of communicating and connecting with people, and as an added bonus, the constant knot in my tummy that had built up over the years, because of my uncertainty, responsibility for everyone and 'walking on eggshells' mentality, was melting away. It was not until the tightness in my tummy had gone that I even realised it was there in the first place – it had just become one of the many things that I had carried around with me and something that I assumed was just how it was.

I came to the point when I realised I was done with the crutch of the 12-step programme. I was sitting in a meeting starting with the accustomed mantra, "My name is Ann-Marie and I am a recovering codependent," and as I said those words, inside my head I started to ask the four questions from Byron Katie's The Work[25] – the first question being: Is it true?

As I did this deep internal self-enquiry, I came to the answer that, no, it was not true for me anymore, it was just another story. I let this settle, and as I did so, I wondered if I was in denial and this was another ego trick, and as such I knew I didn't want to rush into any decisions. I trusted I would find my answer... I emailed my mentor and explained what had happened and how I was feeling about leaving co-da and her reply was short but sweet: "I've been waiting for you to get to this point, Ann-Marie," and that is all I needed to hear. I knew that my gut feeling was indeed correct. She didn't tell me what to do or influence me – she was practising good recovery herself. Thank goodness for healthy people around us, who hold that space and vision for us.

The programme had been a much-needed crutch at that time and was such a great support for me, and I am eternally appreciative of the programme and what I learnt, but I knew it was time to move on. I knew I was capable of standing on my own two feet and, more importantly, walk my own path knowing I had God by my side.

This stage of awakening is crucial for our ultimate freedom. We must learn to trust what we need when we need it and as such be willing to take a step into the unknown, otherwise we may stay stuck in the same old cycle for years.

I have seen this again and again whether in a spiritual sect, religion, programme, therapist or even with a so-called guru. There is no one way, and please be very mindful of anyone who tells you otherwise. It is unhealthy to be dependent upon anything or anyone outside of ourselves and our relationship with our Source. God does not need you to conform to any association or have an exclusive membership or idol – this is just another ego distraction. Dip in, yes, and find what helps and supports you through your journey of awakening, but don't get lost in just one way. Instead trust that each thing that comes your way is but a stepping stone to the journey back home to God.

What have you used to fill your own God gap?

This is the perfect opportunity, if you are willing, to see some of the ways in which you may have given your power away or wanted to be in control of another. We do this from a place of deep acceptance, kindness and compassion for ourselves – we are not trying to nail ourselves to the cross, but free ourselves from the bondage of the illusion that people need to be saved. Relief is the goal and is just around the corner.

Take some time out where you will be undisturbed. Have

a pen and paper handy – light a candle if you so choose and have an intention to open up a Space of Grace. Take a few deep breaths, and little by little drop down into your heart and settle into that spaciousness.

You may wish to use the prayer below, altering anything that does not feel true for you.

Dear God, I am willing to see, with compassion and kindness, the ways in which I have been ego-led into believing I know it all. I understand that I did not perceive my own best interests and I, inadvertently, chose to be the higher power for someone else. I no longer wish to be in control in this way and my heart's desire is to see the way you would have me be and how I can best serve others through your Grace. I am coming to understand that I do not need to fix anyone or indeed preach to them. I will trust you to guide each person home. If you wish for me to be a part of someone's awakening, you will guide me in ways I can be truly helpful, which are in alignment to the laws of the Universe. I look forward to opening up to your Love more, and will see this opportunity as a powerful pathway of growth and part of my awakening journey. And so it is.

Thank you............................ (insert your name)

Tune in and ask to be shown ways in which you have innocently tried to be the Higher Power for someone else. Don't make this a big deal. Just be curious and foster a gentle awareness, and be willing to forgive yourself. I have given a process to use, along with an example below using the situation with my daughter.

Name it using an 'I' statement: I see how I smothered my daughter's growth by living in fear and worrying about her.

See your intention behind it: I wanted to keep her safe and protect her.

The truth: She doesn't need my protection as she is a child of God, eternal, boundless, and has her own inner guidance system.

Letting go: I recognise that to set my daughter free I need to detach from being her 'wise' mother and allow her the opportunity to learn and awaken to her own truth, and just as importantly, her own wisdom.

Offer it up to God: Dear God, I can't do this on my own, please help me. I love my daughter so much and I know your Love is eternal and boundless, and she must return to your arms to be truly free and in alignment.

Forgive yourself: I did my very best with the information I had, and I have come to realise that I inadvertently used my daughter as a distraction from my own inner wounds. I now choose to look after my own counsel and forgive myself for seeing anything else but perfection in my daughter. She has been my teacher and now we are both free.

Wrap a blanket of love around yourself: I am doing so well, I am opening up more and more to love and releasing my old patterns and ways. I Love me – I am proud of me – I am here for me – I am ready to trust you completely.

Dive deeper into your heart and rest in the presence of Love: I lean into Love, I rest in Love, I allow Love to hold me and soothe me. I am a child of God.

Ask if there is anything else you need to be made aware of and then totally hand it over to the Universe: Thank you for this healing and opportunity to grow – I hand everything over to you. Please guide myself and my daughter well – thank you.

Ask your heart: What would you have me do now? I am open to listening to your guidance, God, be you in charge.

Once completed: Give deep thanks and appreciation for the learning opportunity and trust that the next time you feel the pull to control/fix/preach, you will take a conscious breath, relax, pray and ask God's Grace to guide you. You will listen out for the signs, you will trust your intuition and be willing to do nothing until the calling is coming from your heart. If you are meant to do nothing, you will honour this and trust that God has it sorted!

If, however, you feel the calling to share something that is guided by Grace, then let go and allow God to speak through you. You will learn to do this without an agenda or outcome, and to trust that whether or not this person takes on board the information or wisdom that you have shared, you have done your part. You let go of the outcome and hand them back to Love.

Chapter 10

Building Trust and Faith

I hope by now you are beginning to see that the SA is a powerful process and one that unfolds in its own unique way and involves a lot of dismantling of our old identities, as well as accepting the Divine Light that you are. There comes a point on the SA path that asks us to take the next leap of faith and totally surrender to this Source for all our needs, and I mean all!

This next phase involves getting out of our own way and letting go of all the crutches, addictions and go-to fixes we have used to bolster us thus far. We have to get to the point of walking on our own two feet, just as we did as a young child when, for the first time, we let go of our parent's hand and took our first tentative steps. Inevitably there were stumbles and falls, but how else do we learn to figure things out? The lust for life and freedom spurred us on and so we would keep getting back up again and again, feeling the life force pulling us to adventures and a love for life. If, however, we were continually wrapped up in cotton wool or were ridiculed for our stumbles and not shown any love or kindness, it actually embedded fear instead of trust and we eventually lost the trust and confidence of a loving presence, and then sought validation or confidence in something or someone else.

And so it is that on our own SA we need to start building trust and faith in the one and only stable and constant thing that will never leave us comfortless or alone – our Higher Power.

I remember in the early days of my divorce, as I was learning how to walk on my own two feet again, how frightening it felt, because somewhere along the line, I had lost the ability to trust my own strength and inner guidance. I had learnt to fill up my time with action and doing, and had become mostly dependent on my husband and family as my means of entertainment, love and supply.

I vividly remember one particular occasion when the kids were staying with their father, and I was feeling anxious at the prospect of being on my own. I felt an overwhelming feeling of emptiness and inferiority, believing that I was the only person in the world who was on their own, with visions of happy families, lovers and friends everywhere having the best time ever. And there I was with the ego message banging around in my head that I was a total loser, a failure and quite frankly deserving of being all alone.

In desperation I tried ringing a couple of people to offload, but no one answered. The Universe was quite clearly saying to me, "Hey girl, nowhere to run to – it's just you and me." This was not a prospect I relished, and I felt totally bereft at the realisation of having nowhere to run to and nothing to fill the gap with – the void of all voids with Grand Canyon proportions was now staring me right in the face. I knew it was time to face this head on.

Now that I've cleared your schedule, let's talk.
God

I had been learning to connect to my feelings and to acknowledge them, so I tuned into the feeling of emptiness and churning in the pit of my stomach and identified it as loneliness. I owned it and said out loud, "I feel lonely!" I think this was one of the first times I had been brave enough to sit with the overwhelm and not abandon myself through my usual distractions. Instead I knew it was time to just sit with myself in that space and give myself permission to really feel the loneliness for the first time, and as I did, an avalanche of tears poured from my being as I crumbled to the floor, and sobbed deep waves of grief and pain. I was literally and metaphorically on my knees – and this was the deepest level of surrender I had ever dared to experience. When I eventually stopped crying and my body began to find stillness, I looked up from the floor and leant against the side of the bed. There were no more tears to cry, the wailing ceased, my body became silent and everything melted away. A deep, deep sense of serenity and peace filled my entire being as I gave way to the ocean of Love that had eluded me for so long. Wow – I had done it! I was exhausted, but so very alive. I had at last given myself permission to give up the fight, and the hard exterior of protection had melted away.

After that experience, I knew that whatever else happened in my life, I had a way to be with uncomfortable feelings and that I didn't need to run away anymore. The door of the self-imposed prison was now open, and the liberation I felt showed me, without any shadow of a doubt, that my relationship with my Higher Power was intact and always there for me, and with that Love I was capable of coming through any dark night of the soul.

What also transpired was a clearer awareness of how I had been such a diligent spiritual student, striving for enlightenment and so very lost in the searching for some spiritual band aid to make it all better that I had inadvertently just created another ego construct to live by. It's hysterical really, and once I understood the ego's seek and do not find mentality, I began to settle into a much calmer space.

Many of us get stuck in this sticky web of confusion when we are a spiritual seeker and are trying to find the next answer, but what happens in reality is that we just continue down the ego's path blinded by its clever distractions, like a siren luring us on to the rocks again and again. But to be truly free we need to give up the false gods and idols we give power to. We make idols of our job, our religion, our qualifications, our material possessions, our body, our children, our partner, our politics, our food, our phones, our cars, our planet, our money and so it goes on…

A Course in Miracles puts it so beautifully from lesson 140:

> *So do we lay aside our amulets, our charms and medicines, our chants and bits of magic in whatever form they take. We will be still and listen for the Voice of healing, which will cure all ills as one, restoring saneness to the Son of God. No voice but this can cure. Today we hear a single Voice which speaks to us of truth, where all illusions end, and peace returns to the eternal, quiet home of God.*[25]

This is where discernment and radical self-enquiry are so important if we are to transcend the ego's ways. It takes a lot of practice to listen to the voice of Love over the voice of fear, but if we are committed to 'the truth' this really is our only work. We have to wake up each day with a vision of a blank canvas, or as the Zen philosophy encourages 'a beginner's mind', and in my experience, God will guide us to paint the picture and supply all we need to do so. We can then get our hands off the proverbial steering wheel and take our seat on the passenger side and enjoy the ride. Everything you need is already here right now and will continue to be so each day of your life in physical form, because you are always cared for and supported by God. All your needs will be met, and when Eckhart Tolle wrote his book *The Power of Now*, this is exactly what he meant: the 'power' is here NOW, so let's just give up the search.

This is the big one, folks, and can save you many years of fruitless seeking and suffering, and I have seen time and time again, where the know-it-all mentality has actually taken the seeker further and further away from their truth. I don't want that for you, I want you to wake up now, I want you to join me and all the other mighty companions who are increasing the ripple of transformation and saying yes to a Divine and guided life. But you have to stop distracting yourself.

How do you really feel now that I have laid it at your feet? Do you want to be free of the incessant seeking and know that all you need is right here, right now, and that the God of your understanding has never left you? It has patiently been calling you back home and wants to take you by the hand and lead you to a life of utter freedom and bliss, where your fears melt away and your heart beats in tune to the rhythm of Love.

With that prospect just notice what is swirling around in your head or what are you feeling and noticing in your body right now. Be alive with it all – invite it in. Take time to drop down from your ego crazy thinking head and into your beautiful heart. Just sit in the presence and perfection of now, and just notice what you notice. Please give yourself this time to just be a compassionate observer without having to prove or fix anything. Just let any emotions or feeling come to the surface. Then, dear friend, speak it out, voice it to God: "I feel…….. lonely, sad, in pain, ashamed, unloved, not good enough, the spiritual know-it-all, the wise one, guilty, ashamed, etc." Whatever it is, just let it be heard and witnessed in the space of the now. Just let it be as it is… Watch what decides to happen next without judgement or expectation… Be curious and step back a while, and remember to breathe, and know you are loved always.

Once we give our deepest secrets a voice, we can open up to another level of surrender. Nurture, soothe and love yourself exactly as you are, and trust that God has heard you. Then allow the next step to unfold moment by moment. Stay present and feel the life force surging through your body and heart. Feel the aliveness of the present moment and trust that there is nothing to figure out, no more trying to save the world, no more pretending to be something you're not, no more hiding your truth, and then just rest in God. Trust the next step will unfold exactly when it's needed – just be here now.

Welcome Home

In summary, this stage is about being in presence and allowing space for everything to just be as it is. I know this can feel like a massive leap of faith, but little by little, as we detach from the past and the future, and choose to be in the now, life becomes so much more manageable and easier. We come to allow infinite intelligence to create our life and we learn to let go of the how, and instead be guided by Love and ask to be shown discernment between ego's guidance and God's guidance. This requires faith and trust, yes, but ultimately all that you need to do is offer a little willingness and miracle upon miracle will unfold before your very eyes.

What is yours will come to you, so be prepared to hand over your unworthiness and littleness, and ask to be shown your worthiness and magnitude. Through your conscious thought and presence, things will be turned around, and whatever your heart desires will be given by grace and in the perfect way for you.

If you are ready to trust the Universal Laws and wish to create heaven on earth, then be willing to say a massive YES to life, and see the world as a playground not a war-zone. Learn to listen to the hunches and then act with inspiration, and you will see that the action is natural, easy and flowing, it's not pushing, controlling or manipulative. Dramas, conflict and suffering fall away as you commit to opening up even further to the immense capacity you have to shift your life to another level of complete joy. It is a beautiful partnership between you and your Higher Power and this union is a delicious, guided dance of exquisite beauty that will leave you feeling loved beyond words, and all the support you need will appear in the most miraculous ways – effort is not required.

The more you choose this way of being, the more you will come to a place of deep acceptance of yourself, others and the world. You are less reactive and learn to trust that the Universe truly has your back.

Albert Einstein asked a profound question related to this subject. 'Is the universe a friendly place?' and A Course in Miracles helps us to go even deeper with its question, 'What Is the Real World?'

The real world is a symbol, like the rest of what perception offers. Yet it stands for what is opposite to what you made. Your world is seen through eyes of fear, and brings the witnesses of terror to your mind. The real world cannot be perceived except through eyes forgiveness blesses, so they see a world where terror is impossible, and witnesses to fear can not be found.

The real world holds a counterpart for each unhappy thought reflected in your world; a sure correction for the sights of fear and sounds of battle which your world contains. The real world shows a world seen differently, through quiet eyes and with a mind at peace. Nothing but rest is there. There are no cries of pain and sorrow heard, for nothing there remains outside forgiveness. And the sights are gentle. Only happy sights and sounds can reach the mind that has forgiven itself.[26]

Doesn't it sound wonderful – a world where there are no cries of pain or sorrow and all sights and sounds are gentle and happy? It is closer than you think my friend, because it's in your mind, and to live this way we have to be devoted and dedicated to our homecoming by digging a little deeper to see how much we really trust in the Universe/God for ALL our needs. Therefore, please be willing to be open to the following self-enquiry, so that we can flush out any egoic resistance to the real and totally friendly world.

On a scale of 1 to 10 with 10 being the best, how friendly do you feel the Universe/God is?
On a scale of 1 to 10, how much do you trust the Universe/God?
On a scale of 1 to 10, how willing are you to hand your entire life over to the Universe/God?

Take some time to drop down into your heart and breathe deeply for several minutes. Feel the expansion of your chest as you consciously breathe, and if you get distracted just call yourself back to the breath again. After you have relaxed and softened your body, connect to your heart centre, and allow it to have a voice and ask it to reveal to you the truth around your fear and lack of trust in the Universe/God. Don't try and pre-empt, work it all out or have a plan, just trust the process. You may receive immediate guidance, awareness of an old hurt, a painful memory or judgement, or you may not. It's okay either way, but do be prepared to hand your uncertainties, fears and issues over to God/Spirit/Love for healing and forgiveness, and ask to be shown the miracle in this situation. Trust that the answer or guidance will come at the perfect time for you. It's amazing where the messages can be found, it may be a friend who just happens to mention a particular book, it may be a song that comes on the radio with the exact words that inspire or soothe you, it may be a 'random' video clip that comes on and answers your question in the most perfect way, it may be a symbol that you just know is for you, it may be revealed in your meditation or it may be through your journalling or creative expression. There is no limit to the ways in which the Universe will deliver the signs, because you are limitless. You just have to be totally open and receptive to hearing the truth.

Leap and the Net Will Appear (I Promise)

One meditation that helped me, as I was learning to really trust this invisible force, was to visualise myself standing on the edge of a cliff or mountaintop, then to jump off the edge into the abyss. Initially, it did feel crazy and against my natural instincts, even in a meditation, but I knew it was something that I had to do. Every part of my being was telling me to leap and I trusted this inner knowing!! When I did jump, it was the most amazing feeling of freedom. I kept falling down and down and down for what felt like an eternity, but eventually a massive, gentle, loving hand appeared, breaking my fall. It was the hand of God and it lifted me softly back on to solid ground. I felt so safe and liberated, and wanted to jump again and again to the point that I found myself running off the edge with utter glee. I came to know that the old adage of 'leap and the net will appear' was indeed true!

This particular meditation is helping you test, in a safe way, how much you are willing to let go, and I encourage you wholeheartedly to try it for yourself. If it sounds like a blast, do it – if it intrigues you, do it, and if it scares the hell out of you, definitely do it! What have you got to lose?

Full Circle

It seemed that the metaphor of being on the edge and leaping into the unknown was becoming a bit of a theme in my life! It happened at the beginning of my awakening with 'The Falling', as well as the above-mentioned meditation, and then the Universe gave me an opportunity to try it for real.

In the summer of 2019, whilst in the process of writing this book, I discovered the work of Dr Joe Dispenza and was instantly drawn to his teachings. It came at the perfect time to teach me such invaluable leading-edge science-based work. I was inspired to combine neuroscience, quantum physics and spirituality all together, and it was exactly what I needed to open me up on a much deeper level to the quantum field. I hadn't been looking for this; it just came to me and I knew by the way that I felt, that this was to be part of my continued awakening.

I had such a strong message to go to one of his intensive retreats, and even though it was expensive and a big commitment, I just knew I had to go. The first event of his that wasn't fully booked was to be in Mexico at the beginning of December. Spaces were like gold dust, but clearly the Universe wanted me to go and I easily booked my space, to the great distaste of my ego, which had a full-on rampage of why I was a complete idiot who was throwing away money on a whim!! I let the ego have its rampage and tantrum, as I knew it was just an ego backlash, and within 24 hours I was totally calm and so excited at the prospect of this adventure of a lifetime – bring it on, I was fully ready for the next leap of faith!

The week in Mexico involved a lot of meditation, deep inner work and teachings of the power of the mind, quantum physics, the science behind survival and healing. Also included in the week were a couple of 'challenge activities', which were intended to help participants overcome their fight or flight survival pattern, and break old habits and fears.

Ordinarily this would not have been something I would have chosen. In fact, it would have been the last thing I would have done. I certainly wasn't an adrenaline junkie and my default pattern was to stay/play safe! But it seems the time had come for me to override that particular worn-out fear and I was ready to surrender it – gulp.

I'll briefly paint the picture for you – we arrived in our groups at the place where the activity challenges had been set up. It all looked a bit daunting with high-rise frames and places to leap from, left, right and centre, and a plethora of staff with high viz jackets, ropes and hard hats. Our group was guided towards a row of benches, which looked a little friendlier, where our first challenge was to take place. It consisted of a platform, probably about 7ft high or so, and in turn we were to walk up the steps and stand on the edge of the platform, where we were to fall backwards on to a trampoline-like net. This net was held by the rest of our team, and we had all been briefed on how to do that. Our team leader was with us on the bench and supported each person in turn to fall into the net, and at the point we were ready to let go, we were to shout out to our fellow team members, "I am ready to surrender." They then braced themselves ready to catch their fellow teammate replying, "Surrender now."

Watching the first few people of my team do the challenge was an amazing experience to witness. It was so moving to see each person overcome their fears and let go. When it came to my turn I had an army of butterflies surging around in my stomach, along with an understandable sense of uncertainty. This was most definitely out of my comfort zone, and yet I had such a deep desire to leap into the unknown. Standing on the edge of the platform was a pretty hair-raising experience. It felt so counter-intuitive to fall backwards into thin air, and once you are up there it seems a much longer drop than when holding the net below. Our wonderful team leader did an amazing job of getting each one of us into the zone and harnessing our, by now, desire to overcome our old limiting habits. There was such camaraderie, love and support from everyone, which I deeply appreciated, when at last it was my turn.

I have to say it was a pretty amazing experience, and I felt so moved and deeply proud of myself, and it affirmed to me that anything is possible, when we are open and prepared to overcome our limiting mindset. That was just as well, because the next challenge was even more of a heart pounding full-on experience. In for a penny, in for a pound!!

This time it was high and I mean high!! I got hooked up with all the harness gear and a safety helmet ready to climb up a very high structure via a ladder to where a narrow beam was waiting to be traversed. And on top of everything else, halfway along the beam, strategically placed, were oval discs that wobbled when you stepped on them, just to add a little more jeopardy in what was an already full-on extreme experience.

I don't think I have ever been so focused in my life. I called on everything I knew about trust, acceptance and faith, and repeated over and over in my head the mantra: "You can do this, Ann-Marie, I love you," as well as calling on God to hold my hand. I needed all the support and courage I could muster up, as I knew this was the only way I was going get through it. Even climbing the ladder was daunting, but perched on the edge of the beam, with nowhere to go but ahead, was a pretty daunting prospect. I was petrified, but I knew it was time to step forward in complete trust.

The whole experience felt like a dream, like time had stood still and I zoned out everything else around me. I don't quite know how I did it, but I did. I overcame my fear of heights, as well as my old limitations, and came to see that day with greater clarity – the true meaning of mind over matter. It was a truly amazing and profound experience, and one that will stay in my heart to remind me of my unlimited faith in God.

I cannot even begin to put into words the difference in the Ann-Marie who first experienced 'The Falling' all those years ago, to the Ann-Marie who rocked up in Mexico, willing to become the master within and dive into the abyss. It still moves me deeply when I see this transformation and I hope that you will get a sense of the immense potential that you have too – to overcome your own story and step into your utter magnificence and trust. This is what we are doing every day when we are on the SA journey. We are going into the unknown and jumping into the void – the void of unlimited potential.

I am guessing that a few of you, dear readers, may be shouting at the book right now – with words similar to, "Well it's alright for you to say leap, but how the f**k do I do that then?" And I will reply by saying I am just like you, with the same fears, upsets, inferiority and uncertainty, which I know feels like hell. But I took a decision to jump anyway, because I had nothing to lose, and quite frankly I'd had enough of feeling so small and limited. If we just carry on as we are, we will just keep getting the same outcome. It really is your choice, and I am figuring that if you have got this far in the book, there is something in you which is ready to go further than before, and align to who you really are. This book won't do it for you, no it won't, and it may even end up on the shelf with all your other books and look very impressive to the spiritual eye. But I want more than that for you, dear friend, I really do. It's come to the point where it's not just enough to read about it, attend another course, join the enlightened debates, post an inspirational quote on social media and just dream of waking up. It's time to go within, open your heart and be prepared to look at your limiting old beliefs and practise, practise, practise. Enough talking the talk – it's time to walk the walk!

As you dedicate yourself to this level of inner work, you will awaken to someone who can walk in their own skin and love all parts of themselves, to feel truly alive even in the sadness, the anger, the love, the play, the mess, the grief, the passion, the lost and the found. To walk in a strength of knowing you are enough, you are loved and you are eternal, and whatever comes your way you can accept and move through with grace, humility and presence.

That my friend is raw and real and the place I would love to meet you – the naked place – the place where two hearts meet – the place of seeing each other as the Christ.

Out beyond ideas of rightdoing and wrongdoing there is a field. I'll meet you there.
Rumi[27]

The muscle of trust needs to continuously be strengthened and I have found affirmations incredibly helpful for this phase, because when they are said with enough conviction and belief, there is a strong possibility they will manifest into our lives. However, if the affirmation does not fit or resonate 100% there will be doubt in our energy field, and it will be a waste of time and energy. I've experienced this many times in the past and would get all fired up using affirmations, only to feel despondent and drop back into the ego disbelief system when I didn't see an instant result. Repetition is the key because the subconscious mind believes what it is fed without question. If it is consistently being fed the same information over and over again, it becomes a truth in our lives, whether it is something we want or not. The momentum of a thought (energy) will grow if we keep feeding it, and the longer the subconscious continues to hear the same message, the stronger the connection and so it becomes our reality.

It's no good saying for example: "I am healthy and vibrant and full of energy," if you really don't feel it, and you see the opposite in the mirror! You may speak it but not feel it, and the Universe picks up on what you are feeling. Instead you could say something like, "I am open and ready to release old patterns of dis-ease and limitation from my mind and body system, and forgive any grievances or attack thoughts about myself or another. And so it is."

This statement is softer and more manageable, and very soon you will be able to affirm, "I am healthy and vibrant and full of energy" with a certainty like never before.

Your thought process and self-talk are, therefore, so important to be aware of, and once you begin to open up in this way, you can start to train your mind into a more loving way of thinking, and this in turn will start to dismantle the old habit and belief. It's never too late to start and ANYONE can do it – including you!!

In summary, instead of giving energy to the old patterns/ programmes, start to shift your perceptions and focus on the truth instead – the truth being: you are a child of God, you are entitled to miracles, you are Love, you are light, you are innocent, you are whole, you are free, you are blessed. The more you focus on these truths the more the old ego lies will fade away. This is a fact and a spiritual law and this is when the SA journey really starts to get exciting, as we take ownership of the power of our asking, knowing that the Universe always gives in response to our request. We have to continually trust and hand over all things to the Universe and, therefore, it is essential to carve out the time to be present with Spirit in this way.

This phase is a time to assimilate our learning and growth thus far, and a good reminder to refrain from running to another workshop, therapist, guru or training modality for all the answers like before, and instead learn to trust your guidance. It doesn't mean that you won't ever have the need for a teacher, coach or workshop, but what it does mean, is that it will be divinely guided and you will be led every step of the way with ease. The 'I know' mind will be a distant memory, and Divine guidance will be your natural way of living and breathing.

Chapter 11

Moving On and Moving Through

Once we have truly leapt and are committed to our spiritual awakening, the one thing that really won't be at all happy with your progress, is our old friend, the ego. As I am sure you have seen throughout this book, the ego goes from suspicious to vicious the more we choose peace, and it will sit in waiting, dreaming up some seemingly justified guilt trip, drama or catastrophe to scupper us. It feels like the metaphorical bungee cord, which pulls us back once we have reached a certain point of happiness... woosh, back we go, and this ego backlash, can, if we are not careful, make us feel overwhelmed and take us down into another deep hole of darkness again. It's, therefore, crucial to get some distance on these ego distractions, so that we can stay in alignment and not lose our way.

The ego has many disguises and in the beginning of our awakening it can be hard to see them, but the further along the journey we go, the easier it becomes to spot them. Once you can see them for what they are, they will have less hold and fall away a lot quicker.

A Course in Miracles explains that you cannot see two worlds, and the perception of one world (ego) will cost you the vision of the other (God), so we must choose which world we wish to nurture. I would, therefore, like to highlight the subtle ways in which the ego wants to keep you from completely waking up, so that you can have your radar attuned, ready to identify its distorted point of view.

In my experience these are some of the subtler constructs of the ego, which are nonetheless still potent, especially when we have already cleared a lot of the deeper baggage. This is the fine-tuning, so to speak, but just as important to be vigilant of:

- Regret/If only
- I should/could have
- Jealousy
- Apathy
- Depression
- Resentment
- Retaliation
- Why me, it's not fair, here I go again
- I can't do it
- Spiritual superiority/inferiority
- Bodily superiority/inferiority
- Fighting a cause by campaigning or complaining
- Pain in any form

You get the picture!

Please don't give yourself a hard time when you realise you are in the grip of the ego's wily ways, and please do not analyse it to death and try to figure it all out. Notice the word anal in analyse, yes, it's a bummer, but we must forget about getting to the root of it all and instead turn to the perfect plan that is already written for you. You see, nothing happens by accident, and everything and every person that comes into your life is part of the bigger picture put in place for your awakening.

Part of that sacred plan is to get to a place where we can forgive not only ourselves for our perceived errors, but also those whom we have met along the way that we think have done us wrong or acted inappropriately in some way. We are being asked to surrender our perceptions to see only the truth in every person and know, without exception, that everyone is our spiritual brother or sister.

The holiest of all the spots on earth is where an ancient hatred has become a present love.
A Course in Miracles[28]

The Gift of Forgiveness

We will draw unto ourselves many mighty companions, who will bring forth the perfect opportunities not only to forgive and heal, but to practise our new behaviours. They arrive in different forms, some may be fleeting, whilst others may be a lifetime of learning. Either way, we are now much more present and willing to see all relationships through new eyes – the eyes of Love. As this unfolds, we will see the mastery at play, like the perfectly written script, which places the characters in each scene with precision and grace. Each new scene will be a beautiful unfolding of heart-opening experiences, with synchronistic dances aplenty, and these partnerships will also offer great opportunities to extend love, laugh, share, have fun and return to innocence. These relationships may be friendships, work companions, spiritual mentors, partners, children or strangers 'we happen to meet' along the way. There are never any accidents or mistakes on the spiritual path, and every encounter is always a call to Love and part of the greater plan. If we choose to see these opportunities as just that, we can let go of trying to be clever or 'spiritual' and trust a deeper level of non-attachment to the physical form that has shown up in our lives. There is an ease around them, with mutual respect and love, and our spiritual maturity can handle any situations or issues that may come along, as there is a willingness to ride the wave of grace together, with an openness to resolve any misdemeanours or triggers that present themselves. We will, of course, still attract 'challenging' relationships, but this is good news, because it shows us that we still have healing to do and the Universe has brought to us the perfect person with which to evolve and practise quantum forgiveness. This level of forgiveness moves beyond right or wrong, attack or defence – it literally illuminates the perceived darkness and shines the light of pure love on to it. In this light, only the truth is seen and all grievances are transcended.

The forgiveness I am talking about is not how most of the material world see it, which is the conventional way of excusing somebody for a perceived error or wrongdoing, i.e., you have done something 'wrong' (in my egoic eyes) and I (the egoic 'I') will excuse you because, clearly, I am more superior than you, and I am the one who gets to decide on your fate and punishment. From the ego's perspective, we assume that something went wrong and, of course, every judgement from the ego is its futile attempt to keep us separate from Love – no exception here at all.

True spiritual meaning of forgiveness shows us that nothing ever went 'wrong' and God has no need to forgive, for it saw nothing to condemn in the first place. I know this may sound rather radical, because we have been taught the opposite. We have been hoodwinked into living in fear and constantly watching our back, ready to attack or defend the rightness or wrongness of pretty much everybody in the world, as well as ourselves.

There is such a deep mass ego hallucination that wants us to hang out in the judgement arena of superiority, and as soon as there is a sniff of someone doing something wrong or who has dared to behave in a way we don't agree with, they must be punished, belittled and suffer. Let's face it, most of us at some time in our lives have been adamant that Hitler, Gaddafi, Saddam Hussein, the rapist, the murderer and the like, are evil and the scum of the earth, and as such really don't deserve forgiveness in any shape or form. I used to feel so full of utter rage, and be seething with contempt thinking, "How could this happen, why oh why do people behave in this way, they must be taught a lesson, they must be locked up with all the other horrible people in the world," etc. And from the human ego perspective, this seems very justified. However, from a spiritual perspective it is an utter waste of time and energy, which just separates us even more from truth and the Divine within. What an ace card the ego plays here, how cleverly it has come up with the ultimate trap to keep us incarcerated for the rest of our lives. Can you see this, can you see that it actually wants to punish you first and foremost, and, therefore, manifests these projections on to the screen of illusion, labelled as justification? But if you truly wish to be happy, you have to open up just a little, and drop your own defences to see how we are wooed into deeper and deeper separation by the ego, expending hours, weeks and years fighting the good cause and, of course, the ego rubs its hands together with satisfaction.

Meanwhile, God just continues to Love, to Love us all, every damn one of us, and yes, even the 'perpetrator', because Love NEVER ever sees wrongdoing, let alone holds a grudge or deems anyone as punishable. I'm not saying for a moment that we should condone the awful things that happen or that we should hang around with people who are physically or emotionally abusive to anyone and just think that it's okay – no, that would be unkind to ourselves and our brother, but what I am saying is that to be free, we have to let go of the need to punish everyone and judge everything, and practise forgiveness instead.

By grace I live. By grace I am released. By grace I give. By grace I will release.
A Course in Miracles[29]

A Reason, a Season Or a Lifetime

I was attending a three-day coach camp, run by Robert Holden, back in the spring of 2019. I had most definitely been guided to attend this particular weekend and trusted my intuition, as was now becoming the norm for me. I didn't think I had anything particular to learn, but just felt compelled to be there and so I embarked on a mini-break and adventure in London.

I felt so peaceful and receptive and revelled in the fact that I wasn't feeling broken and bereft, as had been the case many times before when I went to workshops. It was just so lovely to be in flow without an agenda.

During one of the first icebreakers, we were asked to go around the room and share our successes from the past week. This felt a natural and lovely thing to do and so I began the exercise with a calm and peaceful heart. The first person I approached was a lady, who I soon discovered really did not want to engage in the exercise at all. She said to me that she was unhappy with the word success. I respected that and suggested that she may like to use the word proud instead, but this didn't work for her either. She made the choice to get herself a cup of tea and return after this exercise was over and I proceeded to carry on with the exercise and enjoyed engaging with new people.

On the next exercise we were asked to pair up with one person. I was sat next to the very same lady who had previously declined to take part and I could feel that I was trying to avoid her, because to be truthful, I really didn't want to work with her again – my preference was to work with someone whom I saw as 'less miserable'!

But, as is always the case, the Universe had other ideas and, you guessed it, we were paired up. My ego was triggered big time thinking, "Oh God, how is this going to work out then?" and I really didn't want to work with her at all. But, I thought, "Well, you know what, here we are and I can resist this or I can trust it," and the bigger part of me knew this had the potential for grace and learning for me. I knew I wanted to be as honest with her as I could, without being defensive or unkind, so I expressed to her how I had felt a little perplexed by the earlier 'rebuff', but realised it was my own ego stuff and judgement. As I was speaking to her, I had a massive light-bulb moment. I realised I (or at least the superior ego I) had put her in a particular camp which separated us. I saw how I had put people in either the 'nice spiritual' camp or the 'not so nice non-spiritual' camp! Wow, what an insight that was, and I have to admit I was quite shocked at this revelation. I had been well and truly wooed by the ego's well-worn path of projection there. Tears started to fall from my eyes and my heart just broke open, as I saw this beautiful woman in front of me, whom I had judged so harshly, and the old filter of separation fell away. Now, all I could see was myself looking back at me and someone who had done their very best. She had inadvertently given me the perfect opportunity to heal an old egoic judgement, which had been playing out for years.

As she continued to share with me, I could really see how much she was hurting and holding on for dear life. She expressed how she had been struggling with the weekend and was still grieving from the loss of her husband. Tears then filled her eyes as she let me into her world for a brief moment. I could see how uncomfortable this was for her and she proceeded to brush away the moment of vulnerability, quickly changing the subject to take the attention away, which I understood, as I too had been in a similar situation when I wasn't yet ready to let down my masks. It's excruciating to do so until we are truly ready. I totally respected where she was at and felt so touched that the Universe had brought us together in this way.

This perfect holy encounter had shone the light on my spiritual snobbery and helped me to see yet another ego lie. Every encounter is an opportunity for Love and healing. Don't get me wrong, I think it is important to be discerning about who we choose to spend our time with, especially when we are in a vulnerable place and in the early stages of our awakening. We do need to be conscious of our boundaries and energy, and only when we have learnt to feel strong in our roots and our connection, are we then ready to show up more in the world and be with new people, as well as heal the stories around our current and past relationships. As we evolve on our awakening journey we will get to the point when nothing and nobody fazes us and we have no need for boundaries, as we have healed the old wounds within, which originally would have triggered us. This is an advanced stage, but ultimately this is the result of doing the continued work of surrender and forgiveness, and I can honestly say that this is the main practice that works every time and on every subject you can imagine.

With this in mind, we can see that forgiveness and surrender are the only logical ways, if we want to be free. Why would you want to be attached to the past, why would you want to prevent yourself from living a beautiful life? Allow yourself to grieve, yes, allow yourself to get mad, yes, but also allow yourself to move on, cut the cords that bind you and remove the heavy chains of attachment and righteousness, and leave them where they belong, in the past. All your power is in the now, and YOU can choose to be free right in this very moment.

Ask yourself this simple question, friend: do you want to be right or do you want to be happy? This is a great question to ask yourself any time you feel judgement or control. You are being asked to drop all defences, drop the knife and stand naked in the power of Love, because the only one that is being hurt is you. Why would you do that? Why would you continue to cut and punish yourself again and again? Because that is what happens every time you hold on to a grievance or choose not to forgive. You, my friend, will be locked in a prison for the rest of your life, and I don't want that for you. I want you to pick up the key and unlock the door. It's time to ask for help, it's time to call to Love and admit you can't do this forgiveness thing on your own, it's time to surrender your way and let the Beloved be in charge.

An Opportunity To Heal

Forgiveness offers everything you want, so here is the perfect opportunity to practise. Bring to mind a person that you have yet to forgive or who has caused you pain. NB. A way to know if you still are carrying a grievance or not is to notice whether when you think of this person all you feel is Love – there is no residue of resentment, contraction or hurt whatsoever.

Once you have brought a person to mind, ask yourself if you are willing, with every cell of your being, to forgive them and see them only as perfect Love? If the answer is no, that's okay, you're not quite ready yet, so my suggestion is to pray for willingness and ask to be shown how to do that.

When the answer is yes, take time to sit in stillness, close your eyes, and with an open heart and empty hands ask your Higher power/Spirit/God/Jesus or the Angel of forgiveness to help you release your burdens and past grievances with this person. Then follow this process:

- In your mind, see the person standing before you and take your time to just breathe and reassure yourself you are doing this process to join in Love, heal your beautiful heart and set each other free.

- Take time to acknowledge the feelings that come up for you when you see this person and write them down. Get real and express it all, no need to be polite here. It is so important to allow the emotions to rise to the surface.

- Once you have written everything down about this person, allow any blame or judgement you feel about yourself to also be expressed. See how much guilt or superiority you have been harbouring within and how unloving that is to you. Clearly this is not in alignment with a loving God and, therefore, separates you from who you really are.

- Next, ask for courage and grace to see the truth in this

person, to see beyond the veil that they are wearing, and then very gently reach out your hands and tenderly hold their face whilst softly looking into their eyes and say SLOWLY:

I want to see who you really are.
Thank you for this opportunity to show me the truth and see you as my mirror.
Thank you for agreeing to be part of my awakening and gifting me with this moment to embrace true forgiveness.
You are pure love.
You are completely innocent.
You are guiltless and perfect just as you are.
You are blessed.
I love you with all my heart.
I wish you only joy, peace and happiness.
Thank you.

- Gently remove your hands from their face, and relax into peace and take a few moments to come back to your own heart again.
- Then imagine a beautiful column of golden light surrounding them. Allow this light to expand and grow bigger and bigger with each breath that you take, until it eventually fills up the entire room. Then in your own heart, imagine a beautiful bright beam of light radiating outwards that joins with the column of light before you.
- Take a few more conscious breaths and feel a never-ending flow of love pouring out of your heart towards this person. Pray for healing for you both, and if you feel any remaining resistance, ask Spirit to help you see this differently. You may then wish to see yourself embracing this person before they dissolve into the light.
- Ask God to place a healing balm over your heart as you

too dissolve into the light.

- Finally, trust the miracle of forgiveness, trust Spirit will free you from the illusion that there was anything to forgive in the first place, trust that you chose this person to help you awaken, and remember God only sees the LOVE that you both are. You are one – he/she is your brother/sister.

If you feel any residue of resentment or anger, it's okay. Just give yourself permission to feel it. It is so important to allow it to be expressed in a way that works for you, crying, writing it down or beating a pillow, etc. Please do not be ashamed of your anger or your feelings. Feelings are meant to be expressed, and anger is a natural emotion that is triggered when we are in fear and it needs an outlet. Just because we are spiritual does not mean we do not still feel heightened emotions, so don't do a spiritual bypass – be real. Know that you can do this exercise as many times as you need to, and pray for ultimate peace and acceptance.

True alchemy is turning the heavy burden (lead) into the sparkling gift (gold). Each broken heart or misdemeanour was a true treasure that taught you clearly what you really want and deserve. How would you know what you want to be different in your life without this gift, how would you have refined the desires of your heart, and how would you be the person you are today without this learning opportunity? Open up the treasure chest of forgiveness and see the gift that awaits you. There is no need to wait until you are on your deathbed to discover it; peace is available now. Each time you forgive, another light in heaven shines brighter, which illuminates us all.

Wherever you are in this moment feel it fully – get mad, get sad, ask for help so you can move through your feelings; and as you do, you'll begin to feel even more connected to yourself and your life. Stay present without trying to work it out or make yourself wrong.

Keep it simple and you won't get so overwhelmed by the future. You are enough now and you don't have to know all the answers. You never will. You don't have to be perfect as a human being because as a Divine being you already are.

Anna Grace Taylor[30]

Seeing Beyond the Illusion

So, my friend, if you desire true freedom, your only work is to forgive anything that disturbs your peace. Furthermore, this doesn't just involve forgiving people, but anything you see outside of you that you think shouldn't be happening, such as war, a pandemic, cancer, breaking a bone, missing the bus, your favourite football team losing the game or even a rainy day.

This is a high level of spiritual metaphysics, but I can assure you that it is the key to true happiness, and has changed my life beyond belief. The more I choose to forgive, the more I feel a joining with Spirit, which means I can just get on with the business of loving life, loving my fellow man and loving what is.

I believe that forgiveness is as important as, if not more than, eating a healthy diet, keeping fit, sleeping well or education. Yes, that's how important it is and I have seen miracle upon miracle when people have truly embraced this level of forgiveness. I would highly recommend you bring it into your daily practice, and it's something I use pretty much any day I find myself separated from Love – if you feel guilt, blame, judgement, attack, defence, comparing, criticising, complaining, anger, frustration, boredom or lost/preoccupied with the past or future, etc., it is the perfect opportunity to practise forgiveness.

Daily Forgiveness Practice:

1) Acknowledge/notice when you are out of your alignment/ peace and have judged a situation or person – even if it's just a minor irritation.

2) Stop and accept that you must have separated from Love and seen through the eyes of the ego not Spirit.

3) Ask yourself, "Do I want to be right or do I want to be happy?"

4) If you want to be happy, then choose to take a few moments to offer the grievance/misdemeanour to your Higher Power and admit that you can't do it on your own.

5) Imagine placing the 'issue' on the altar to God (or some people prefer to imagine placing the issue on to a golden platter instead) and then hand it all over to Spirit, praying for a miracle and to see only the truth.

6) Once you have let it go, trust that your prayer has been heard and come back to the stillness of your heart.

7) Be humble enough to get out of your own way and how you think the miracle and healing will occur. That is not your business; your only work is to be open and receptive to the guidance that will surely be followed by Spirit.

8) Say "Thank you" and "I Love you" to God and then let go.

9) Get on with the rest of your day, trusting the healing has already occurred.

10) Continue with an attitude of Love in all your encounters, including with yourself!

11) Repeat as often as you need to.

Eventually we will be up for forgiving the whole world, because the world you see is just a projection of your mind. If you see a problem 'out there', it is actually coming from within you, because God did NOT create the world you see, he created only Love and, therefore, if you see anything apart from perfect Love, you have seen through the eyes of the ego. Furthermore, the world does not need saving, because, just like you, it is already whole and complete; and as you accept who you really are, so you will see the truth reflected out in the world. Then, my friend, you have truly arrived in a place of freedom, and all you will want to do is sing this joyous melody from the top of the mountains with utter glee, just like the birds, who unapologetically sing their sweet song every day.

As a result, our spirits are lighter and brighter, and we seem to look and act younger with a natural playfulness, curiosity and innocence. This energy is boundless and others feel it too, and just our total presence and unwavering knowing of the truth is enough to make a difference. This is all powerful and Love just pours forth.

Remember, that you don't need to do this on your own, keep praying and asking for the help you need. The Universe wants to work with you and support you in every situation. Always be mindful of asking, "What is this for?" The answer is always, to extend Love, be it a telephone call, cooking a meal, shopping, working, interacting with another, etc. If the intention is to teach only Love, what more could you want! Just turn up each day and allow it all to unfold and always keep reaching out to other mighty companions to support you too.

Grievances are completely alien to love. Grievances attack love and keep its light obscure. If I hold grievances I am attacking love, and therefore attacking my Self. My Self thus becomes alien to me. I am determined not to attack my Self today, so that I can remember Who I am.

A Course in Miracles[31]

Chapter 12

A Guiding Light

For those of you who are committed to following your true path, there comes a point when an even deeper calling comes knocking at the door. And that calling is the only reason we are really here – to share our Love, wisdom and God-given gifts as a 'teacher'.

A teacher of God is anyone who chooses to be one. His qualifications consist solely in this: somehow, somewhere he has made a deliberate choice in which he did not see his interests as apart from someone else's. Once he has done that, his road is established and his direction is sure. A light has entered the darkness. It may be a single light, but that is enough. He has entered an agreement with God even if he does not yet believe in Him. He has become a bringer of salvation. He has become a teacher of God.

They come from all over the world. They come from all religions and from no religion. They are the ones who have answered. The Call is universal. It goes on all the time everywhere. It calls for teachers to speak for It and redeem the world. Many hear It, but few will answer. Yet it is all a matter of time. Everyone will answer in the end, but the end can be a long, long way off. Each one begins as a single light, but with the Call at its centre, it is a light that cannot be limited.

A Course in Miracles[32]

We can see that when I say teacher, it may not look like a conventional teacher, but nonetheless we are teaching by way of example, by living a life devoted to Love and expressing the Divine within us, because it can't help but be shared. This may be in numerous ways, such as therapy work, writing, facilitating, creating, coaching, philanthropy, entrepreneurship, healthcare, as well as in our day-to-day lives, by offering a smile to a stranger, keeping calm in a tricky situation, offering a safe haven of Love when someone is troubled or simply seeing the truth in someone, when they have forgotten who they are.

Previous awakened teachers have been revered, as well as scorned, for their unapologetic inner knowing. Jesus, the Buddha, Ramana Maharshi, Mother Teresa, Gandhi, Martin Luther King to name but a few and, of course, we are blessed to have many modern-day spiritual teachers and mystics, who have heard the calling and continue to help mankind wake up in their own unique way – the way that is guided by Spirit.

Equally there are many awakened beings living a very 'normal' life, but in an extraordinary way. They are walking the walk, and touching the hearts of many in every country on the planet without any obvious recognition at all. They are the quiet ones living in presence and grace and shining their light in all that they do. They may sit on the bus next to you, serve you in a restaurant, have created multimillion enterprises, walk past you in the park or saved your life after an accident. These earth Angels are tuned in and true to themselves, but not deemed as 'spiritual teachers'. They are living and creating from the heart and have learned how to live a fulfilling and guided life in their own way.

They are not 'perfect', for that is not the goal of awakening. They are just turning up each day and extending the love, truth and guidance of their heart, in a humble, transparent and honest way. God isn't looking for perfection, as that is purely an egoic construct. God just wants you to join with your brother/sister and welcome him/her into the arms of love and continue the everlasting ripple of peace and serenity.

Don't get hung up on how, where or when you will do this. Just get out of your own way, take the time to be still and rest in

God. It's in the stillness that you will be aware, not in the doing. Once the awareness comes, you are then gently guided down the path of truth, where all things will unfold in Divine timing.

Heaven On Earth

The simple state of desireless contentment is all we need to cultivate and this, my friend, is the place where we meet God. This is the road less travelled, and as we continue down this pathway, the radical honesty that ensues may shock others, especially those still in the material world of illusion. We may be labelled as selfish or arrogant, but if we are willing to open our hearts, we will come to see that going beyond 'normal' is the only way to freedom, and if it is guided by Love, how can it be wrong?

Just remember to forgive everything that comes up along the way, and say yes to your mission here on planet earth, as one who now steps forth with an intention to shine their light. As you say YES, you carry this light in your beautiful heart without apology, justification or explanation. It needs to be shared and not hidden anymore. You are meant to shine and live a life of utter delight and joy. There is a limitless supply available to you, and there is nothing that is out of your reach. We are not meant to suffer, and the world is waiting for someone just like you to turn up. So be bold and commit to being a beacon of light, to being the light of the world. This is exactly what I have chosen, and why this book has been born and gifted through me, to those who are awakening and wanting another way. I said yes. I pray you will too.

Thank You

Thank you, dear friend, for travelling this path into the kingdom of heaven with me and for being one of the few who are brave enough to listen to the calling. Thank you so much for saying yes to yourself, thank you for turning up. Thank you for being willing to lose yourself to find yourself, thank you for falling apart to rebuild yourself, and thank you for listening to the ancient wisdom of your soul and singing its song.

Together we have asked the meaningful questions, searched our souls, refused to conform and fit in, and dared to dissolve our human identity to discover our true essence. This continued dedication has helped us build mastery over our limiting patterns and teach by example, without any need to preach.

Thank you also for being my mighty companion and walking by my side on this awesome journey of awakening. Even though our paths may never meet in physical form, I know our souls are energetically connected throughout all of time in the quantum field, and our hearts will beat in the rhythm of the One Divine Truth. The Celtic tradition has a beautiful term for this, Anam Cara (Anam meaning Soul and Cara meaning Friend), who was a person that acted as a teacher/spiritual guide and in whom one could share their hidden and intimate world with.

My appreciation of you and all those who have crossed my path on this amazing journey is simply beyond words. I am eternally grateful to have had the opportunity to share just a little of what it takes to wake up, and I bow down with tears in my eyes to you all, as I prepare to write the final words of this book, a book I never thought I could write or believed was even possible. I have learnt so much through this process. Everything that happened to me, and brought me to my knees, was needed and necessary to wake me up. I have emerged from the cocoon and claimed my inheritance as a child of God, and allowed the shy and inferior little girl to blossom and find strength and peace within. This is far beyond anything I could have ever imagined, but imagination is a powerful tool as John Lennon so beautifully shared all those years ago in his iconic and mind-blowing song *Imagine*.

So, my friend, let's make a vow together right now, to live in peace, to join as one, to blossom and bloom and share our beautiful fragrance to the world without apology. This commitment to truth will grow every day, and our roots will go deep and strong, watered by the gentle droplets of love and compassion from the Beloved. This is not the end, it is just the beginning. Step forward now, with love in your heart and trust in every step that you take.

Fly free, beautiful soul, and shine, shine, shine!!
I Love you, I honour you, I bless you.
Ann-Marie x x x

Slow...

I breathe deep into spaciousness and exhale into life
Surrendered in your Love
In awareness and presence
To slow down, to slow it all down

I see nothing, and seek no more
Revelling in utter perfection
My whole essence swimming in an ocean of love
Melting, melting, melting

Slow down I want the world to know
To know this richness of simplicity
To know your pure divinity
To let go the goals and internal war

To stop keeping score
To speak of truth so raw
To just slow down and stop the search
To reach no where, to know no thing

Such simple splendour
Such sweet delight
That comes, but from the one true light
I am undone in you, I am ...

Ann-Marie Marchant

Transcript of Interviews

The following transcripts are of interviews I conducted during the summer of 2019. I asked each person similar questions regarding the SA process and how that transpired for them, along with insights and inspiration that may help those who are awakening. I pray that they touch your heart and show you how, with courage and commitment, the SA is a journey that will be worth taking and will raise you up to new dimensions, and a life of purpose and love.

The information is set out in a simple form based on the talks that we had and, therefore, may not be completely grammatically correct, in chronological order or verbatim, but please trust that the message and intention behind them is pure, transparent and radically honest.

Enjoy!

Sarah Cox

Sarah came into my life when I was falling apart and on the edge. She was the first person who truly saw me and who informed me that I was having a spiritual awakening. Her deep knowledge and unwavering connection to truth has helped hundreds of people wake up and find inner peace. She is a natural psychic and has always had many spiritual experiences, which culminated in her decision to train as an Interfaith Minister, being ordained in 2007. She created her company, Zephorium, without a business plan and trusted only her inner guidance to build an award-winning aromatherapy skincare and fragrance collection, based upon energy attraction and positive thinking.

Without her I would not be the person I am today – she has helped me beyond words and I am eternally grateful for her faith in me and for the light that she shone to guide me home.

What was your experience of a Spiritual Awakening?

The first stage of awakening was the dark night of the soul, when I came to a point of realising that I couldn't be here the way I had been living – I either wanted to go (die) or change it – it was very loud. I had been ignoring it for ever. I had a business, a partner and a home, and then I hit the deck: my partner left me and my business was closed by the bank overnight. All support was gone and I felt like a complete failure – that was my rock bottom.

I was on antidepressants, and many times I would get in the bath, sometimes for up to seven hours, thinking what is the point in getting out. I lived in a high state of anxiety all the time, had ME and was constantly ill, had a lot of sensitivity to different foods, such as wheat and dairy, and ended up having several operations and visits to hospital. I remember being in hospital one day and said if there is a God, I want to be helping other people, because what is the point in being here and feeling so awful all the time. I made a vow – "I want to be worthy and in service if I am going to carry on living" – and then everything fell apart.

I was never really happy, and experienced a painful childhood. I ignored all my feelings and had no idea of who I was or what I wanted. I was always very psychic and aware of energies, but it was not accepted in my family.

[I ended] up in a dark and deep depression for two years. One Christmas I felt so lonely and desperate, thinking, what is the point in going on? I remember going into a shop and feeling utterly worthless and suicidal, a lady saw me and smiled at me, and that smile stopped me from killing myself. She will never know what she did for me, but that smile saved my life, I bless her all the time. I realised that it was the little things on the journey that made a big difference.

I was recommended a book on positive affirmations – it said things like you are a beloved child of God – you are Loved and I would think, "What a load of shit, how could I be a child of God, when I feel like I want to kill myself all the time." I found Louise Hay's book, *You Can Heal Your Life*, and it felt like my bible and I read it all the time. Back in the 80s and early 90s there wasn't much information around awakening, spirituality and metaphysics, and I realised I would have to create the community and people I wanted in my life.

My GP referred me to a counsellor, a lady called Anne, who quite literally saved my life, because she saw who I truly was. It was two years of difficult counselling, and during this period, she suggested that I go on an anger management course, which I did, and by the end of the day I was on the floor with overwhelming emotions. The person who was running the course suggested that I would benefit from some bodywork as well and I subsequently met an amazing bodyworker called Jan. In the first session she commented on how much tension

I was carrying around, and after the massage, I came out in a rash and couldn't get out of bed or walk properly for three days. When I called her up to ask her if this was normal, she said no, not really, and it was then that I realised how much trauma I was carrying.

What also emerged during that period of time, whilst working with Jan, was that it started to open up my psychic abilities again. However, it felt so overwhelming as I had suppressed it for so long, and during one particular session, whilst feeling very relaxed, I saw a shadowy figure in the room – I said to Jan what I could see and she said why don't you invite them in. I did this and a man walked through the closed door – he came around to the bed, stood at the side of me and put his hands into my body and opened each chakra one by one, starting at the base of my spine, and by the time he had finished, it felt like the top of my head had been blown off! It was terrifying and a total shock, which took me six months to, as I put it, screw the top of my head back on. I came to understand later, that it was a kundalini awakening experience, but I wouldn't necessarily recommend it to happen so quickly, as it was so intense, but that is how it happened for me.

I eventually went to the College of Psychic Studies in London and said to the receptionist, "I'm either mad or psychic," and she said to me, "Oh, darling, let's see then whether you are mad or psychic." I went on to train with a wonderful medium for two years, which helped me lose my fear and realise that I was indeed psychic, and I went on to be a stand-up medium.

As I started to feel better, I decided to come off the antidepressants, which was a very frightening concept for me, as I thought that I couldn't survive without them, but I did.

I went on to train to be a counsellor and that was an utter revelation; it was wonderful to be able to share in a group and I could see what this could do for other people. I had to learn to embrace the light, because I had always been in the darkness. I gradually needed to learn to integrate the two, and once, whilst I was facilitating an Angel/psychic development workshop, I felt Archangel Michael step into my body and say to me that I am one with you, we are all the same. It was very overwhelming at the time, but it seemed all my experiences of awakening were extreme.

It's been a gradual awakening over many years, which has got me to the point of now knowing the truth of God. It is a completely unshakable knowing of stability, security, love, safety, expansion and joy. The word God is man-made and somehow seems too small in comparison to the feeling I experience.

What would be the one tip you would say to those who are awakening?

Just start, put one foot in front of the other, and the minute you send out an intention/vow, like I did when I was lying in the hospital bed, know that you then have to let go of the steering wheel and let the universe be in charge, because you are the universe.

Find amazing people to talk to and I would encourage the willingness to be vulnerable and honest, because we are all hiding. Everything that we are longing for is the other side of our resistance. It's essential to have the right support.

The thing we really need to watch is authenticity. There are so many people in spiritual addiction, who give their power away to gurus, etc. We need to be surrounded by friends who call us to accountability and who are willing to say how it is, even at the expense of losing the relationship. The young ones are leaping in fully awake and we will not have a clue what is going on, because they are light years ahead of us. Autism is the way – they are totally awake, they are always right. They are sublime in their honesty, they can see through all the crap.

We all have an internal guidance system and we need to trust it. If you read a book, take what you need from it, but don't make the author a guru – trust what is good for you.

What books would you recommend?

I always have Abraham-Hicks, Michael Newton and Dr Joe Dispenza by my bedside, but trust what is right for you. It doesn't matter what gets you to your freedom, they are all just stepping stones.

Contact Details:

Email: info@zephorium.com

Web: www.zephorium.com

Fb: @zephorium Instagram: zephoriumsoultonic

John Campbell

John came into my life as a result of a prayer to have a male friend and equal. He was hosting a Course in Miracles' study group in Brighton, East Sussex, and when he came to pick me up to take me to the first meeting, I could not have imagined what a healing and fun journey we would share together. We have remained friends ever since and I am truly thankful for all the love, laughter, joy and wisdom that John brings to my life and to the world. He most definitely walks the walk, and together with his dear wife, Annie, has created groundbreaking teachings around sacred union and sex. He is also an international and inspirational speaker who captivates audiences with his wisdom and humour. His specialist subjects are relationships, parenting, Law of Attraction and A Course in Miracles.

What were the first steps of your Spiritual Awakening?
I had a business fail on me, was drinking heavily, was in a toxic and unhappy marriage, and living a wild and risky life. One day after going on a bender, a friend's wife, who could see what was going on for me, gave me a book and said this might help you. The book was *You Can Heal Your Life* by Louise Hay. I thought she was completely nuts, and the book was all a load of codswallop. I wasn't quite ready, but on another occasion whilst at the airport in Nigeria, with a raging hangover, feeling very hot, sweaty, dirty and utterly miserable, I came across another book called *The Power of Positive Thinking* by Dr Norman Vincent Peale. I bought the book and I wrote in the front, "I drink too much, my marriage is a sham, I'm unhappy and I want to change." I dated the page and believe that that was my conscious call for help.

On another occasion, whilst in Nigeria, we stopped in traffic, and as I looked outside, I saw a stall selling books. I spotted a copy of the bible and I asked the driver to pull over, and I bought the book. I was so drawn to it, and what particularly attracted me was the fact that it had all Jesus's words in big red print and this was the only text in the book that I read. I had always been intrigued by Jesus, because I knew how much he loved little children, and as a child I certainly didn't feel loved.

On another trip to the airport to go back home to the UK, I felt like there was someone else in the car and a voice said to me, "Phone Terry when you get back home." Terry and I used to be big drinking buddies and we hadn't been in contact for 12 years. The last time I did see him, I noticed how well he looked, which he told me was as a result of hitting his rock bottom, whilst in hospital with liver poisoning and being read his last rights. He went on to attend a rehab programme and stopped drinking completely.

I thought he was crazy and couldn't wait to get away from him. However, that memory stayed with me, and now feeling so unhappy myself, I knew I had to contact him again. I told him how I had been feeling and he laughed saying, "I knew you would contact me eventually, because I saw how bad things were when we last met." I asked him why he hadn't said anything to me at the time and he said, "I knew you weren't ready to hear it." Now ready, he gave me the telephone number of the treatment centre he had been to and told me to phone them, and it would change my life.

I didn't do it right away and told my wife that I thought I had a problem and that I was an alcoholic. I stopped drinking and smoking immediately, but still didn't phone the number. After several weeks I was sitting in my office feeling awful because, unbeknown to me, all my repressed pain, which the addiction of alcohol had covered up, was now starting to come out.

The voice came back again telling me to phone the number. I had it in my pocket, so I called them and explained how I was feeling and then I started to tell them my life story, and after a short period of time I started crying and the voice at the other end of the line said, "Don't worry, John, everything is going to be alright." I went into rehab and that was the start of my awakening.

Whilst in the centre at one of the early lectures, the counsellor said to us, there are 26 people here today, within two years, going on past statistics, only 10 of you will be here – do you want to be one of the 10 or the 16? Right there and then I said to myself, I want to be one of the 10 and I committed to this programme wholeheartedly. I started to read the *Big Book*, which blew my mind; it was the first spiritual book I had ever read. After seven weeks I came out of the centre and was hungry for any more literature that I could get my hands on, and I got to the point, after two years, where I had to stop reading for a while, as I couldn't take in any more information.

As I continued down the path of sobriety, images and visions from my past started to emerge, which brought up a lot of suppressed feelings and emotions, along with immense fear. I spoke to my psychiatrist about this and he asked me when I had first started drinking. I told him it was at the age of twelve, when my mother got me drunk. He went on to explain that when you have your first experience like this, at such a young age, it stops your emotional growth, thus suppresses all your natural feelings. Consequently, all the repressed emotions are stored away, and only when the alcohol is eventually stopped, does it give the opportunity for them to come out. I cried for months on end – it was a great release.

I had a very abusive home life as a child and I felt very lonely. My mother was always drunk and my father was away at work. My mother used to take me with her to shoplift; she would distract the shopkeeper and I would fill the bag. Once I came out of the shop, I was showered with love, but, of course, this was not a healthy love. I remember walking to school one morning on my own and looking up in the sky thinking, there has to be more than this. I also used to contemplate dying and what it would be like to die; the thought of nothingness was unbearable to me.

Once I started to feel more confident and my self-esteem began to grow again, I wasn't prepared to take any of the crap that I had put up with beforehand from my wife and business partner. I started to stand up for myself and eventually I walked away from both my marriage and business. Lots of people couldn't understand what was happening to me, and my friends said I had been brainwashed, and I said yes, I needed my brain washing!

I continued to go to AA, read the *Big Book* and work with a sponsor. The *Big Book* said that the alcohol was just a symptom of a far deeper problem, and I decided that if that was the case, I wanted to get to the deeper problem. The book also said that AA is a bridge to normal living and we acknowledge that we know but a little, and God will reveal more to us when we are ready. I thought that was very profound, and I became open to everything and wanted to heal myself.

I understood the principle of 'ask and it is given' and the next step for me was shown whilst attending an AA convention. A woman asked me to dance and I said no, I don't feel very well. I knew it was a lie and I went up to my room, lay on the bed, and looked up at the ceiling and thought, why can't I get on a dance floor without any alcohol? The next day I went to college, where I was training to be a counsellor, and a fellow student came up to me and said, "John, you've got to read this book *Healing the Child Within* by Charles Whitfield." When I read the book, I realised why I couldn't get on the dance floor, I had been given the answer to my question.

I knew this was my next step and I wanted to find the best inner child healing course that I could. A week later, I came across an ad in a spiritual magazine advertising The Hoffman Process, which was endorsed by John Bradshaw, saying that this is the finest inner child healing course there is. What topped it for me, was the fact that I was in the middle of reading a book called *Healing the Shame That Binds You* by the very same John Bradshaw! The next question I had, was, where is the course? I found out they were based in Arundel, and Arundel was the place that I used to run away to when I was feeling overwhelmed as a child. I took this as a clear sign and knew I had to do it! I phoned them up and booked on to the next course immediately. It was a transformational experience, and after completing it, I could be found dancing everywhere I could, I had let go of the shame!

I still had a lot of fear, but I kept healing myself, attending courses, workshops and several training modalities. Whilst co-counselling with one of my buddies on my counselling course, I spotted the book *A Course in Miracles* on her table. I said to my buddy, "I would like to have some miracles," and bought the book. I started to study the book, as well as attend a Course study group. I was totally committed to the Course and knew it was my inner calling, and the feeling of searching completely left me.

Did you experience the 'know it all stage'?

Absolutely, I pissed off a lot of people, but the good thing was, it sorted out who my good friends were and who were not. I became more discerning about who to share things with and eventually left behind the spiritual arrogance, but know I needed to go through that stage.

All of this brought about great awareness and I learnt that the only lack was a lack of connection, all the other lacks are just a mirror of an inner lack of connection. That connection is my intuition (inner teacher) and inner knowing.

I feel blessed, because I had such good teachers and therapists; it's so important to get the right help. It's also healthy to know when it's time to move on and not stay stuck in the same thing.

A good example of this was when I was in the treatment

centre, I used to go to church each Sunday, I loved it. I got stuck in and helped in many areas, but after a year or so when leaving the bible study group, I was feeling some doubts about this being my path and I asked God for a sign. The next day the priest phoned me up and said that he felt I should spend less time with my recovery friends and more time around "us Christians" – I knew that was my sign and said thank you to God. That was the last time I attended that church or saw the priest again. There was no animosity whatsoever, he was a lovely guy, but I knew it was time to move on and then that's when I found The Course.

I also came to accept that some people will leave my life and that's okay, and I also understood that what people think of me is not my business, but what I think of them is up to me and my only job is to love them.

Awakening for me is being aware of my feelings on a day-to-day, moment-by-moment basis. I make an intention at the start of the day to practise meditation, spiritual reading and joining with my wife to make Love and join with God. We also both pre-pave our day and are mindful of recognising any judgements, and as soon as we spot them we forgive them, as well as ourselves.

God is a perfect bookkeeper, everything is in balance. There are no debts in the spirit world.

If I don't follow my heart's desire and if I'm not true to myself, then life/the Universe will take the action for me and it's always more uncomfortable.

What nugget would you offer to someone who is just awakening?

Start noticing your feelings and then trust them. Take baby steps and know that if it doesn't flow it's not meant to go. It doesn't mean give up on your dreams, it just means that that particular path was not meant.

Everything is a gift.
You are innocent.
Be totally honest.
Remember to have fun and laugh.
Never give up on love.

Contact Details:
www.wetalkaboutsex.com
www.MiraclesRock.com
Instagram = 1) ajtalkaboutsex & 2) johncampbell9988
Twitter = 1) @AJTalkAboutSex & 2) @MiraclesRock

Books:
The Secret of Intimate Relationships – John Campbell
CURRENTLY IN DEVELOPMENT: Dr Annie & John Campbell of East Sussex in the UK are working with Fearless Literary to develop *SoulSex at 70 (or Any Other Age)* that will summarise their work as spiritual sex educators.

Annie Campbell

Not only is Annie a best-selling author, but she is an internationally recognised and widely published authority on the rapidly developing science of neuropsychology. She had a distinguished career with the BBC as a producer/director and later formed her own film-making company, which won a BAFTA for its series on death. She now works alongside her husband, John, as the co-founder of "We Talk About Sex", which supports couples and singles to learn another way of experiencing the sexual union.

I first met Annie through my friend, John Campbell, at the Love Seminar that I was hosting. They had been a couple for a year or two and met through their shared interest in A Course in Miracles. I gradually got to know Annie and subsequently was asked to be the minister for their wedding. Annie is such an open and engaging person, with a deep wisdom and verve for life, and she just seems to look younger and younger each year as she practises the principles of the Course, as well as other spiritual practices. Her gentle yet clear approach to spirituality and science is so refreshing and inspiring to me.

What is your understanding of a Spiritual Awakening?
It means becoming who I really am, and being authentic and at peace with anything that happens.

I was a pragmatic scientist – and believed when you were dead you were dead. I studied DNA and was a geneticist. Anything spiritual was woo woo to me, and when I was younger I became an atheist.

My husband, Bill, was dying with cancer and he wanted to die at home. He had come to peace with his dying, and somehow, he transferred that peace to me. The day he died was a bright sunny June day – I felt his heart stop and then he stopped breathing. I was totally at peace and then I saw a very bright light leave his body – I had no idea what it was. I knew it was not my imagination.

At that time, I wanted to die because we had been together 27 years and he was my best pal – we did everything together. I felt torn apart and for the first time I was on my own and had no idea who I was. I'd had such a good life until this point and loved everything I did. I had never suffered from depression, but for the first time I was now in the grip of it.

I started to read up on what I had experienced the day when Bill died, and I realised I had been gifted with seeing his spirit leave his body. I came across the book *The Power of Now* by Eckhart Tolle, and in it, he spoke about A Course in Miracles. I was very curious about this book and bought a copy. The lessons in the Course changed so many things in my life. One example – I have a sister who is very sick and has been labelled paranoid schizophrenic and as such 'very dangerous' – she would take a knife to me several times. Her son would not let me go there on my own, but when I started to do the Course, instead of challenging all her fantasies and how she saw the world, I just accepted it all, which changed everything. Now I can go and see her and she is delighted to see me. I realised that through practising the principles of the Course and using forgiveness and Love I could de-programme my ego and old triggers.

I had a hiccup though, which really shook me up and brought a much-needed sledgehammer to immerse me deeper on my spiritual journey and to help me remove the old programming in my mind, which had been set like concrete. I met and fell in love with another man, Mike. We moved in with each other and were having a trial period to see if we wanted to get married. I came home one day and found him dead.

I was so angry with both Bill and Mike for leaving me and dying. I eventually had to learn to forgive them and, of course, to forgive myself.

I had focused a lot on my work and this had been one of the distractions I had used to escape the pain I had been going through. I loved my work and a lot of people depended on me, but I used it to escape and was totally unaware of the spiritual side of me.

It's taken a lot of time and practice to open up to the space of Love and God, but I am now also aware of my guidance while working and don't use it to escape anymore.

I became completely committed to my spiritual practice and eventually found A Course in Miracle's study group, and it was so good to connect with other people. My brother thought I had gone woo woo, but I felt happier. The Course eventually led me to meet my current husband, John – we were destined to meet and have a wonderful life together and support each other, as well as share the things we have learnt together.

I am now comfortable with the word God and I know it is just a symbol – God is ineffable and you can only feel it and experience it. I know that my mind is outside of my body and my body is a creation of my mind and everything that happens to me I ask for. I believe we are the creators of our reality, because I have experienced it. I could never believe in sin, it didn't make sense to me.

I love Abraham-Hicks and Alan Cohen too, both of whom are so accessible.

I aim to live my spiritual practice every day and connect but, of course, I forget, although now I can recognise the feelings and choose to look within to see what my trigger is.

Tools I now use:

Daily appreciation
Meditation
Principles of A Course in Miracles
Law of attraction

Living in the moment

Mantra – one example is: Thank you very much, I have no complaint whatsoever.

I feel I have the secret to life now. It's a very exciting time to be alive.

What little nugget would you offer to someone who is on the journey or who has had a traumatic event like yourself...?

Key for me was to learn to let go of the criticising, judging and trying to control things, instead I use forgiveness for everything.

Focus on harmony and connection, not differences.

Trust you are always looked after in all areas.

Contact Details:

www.wetalkaboutsex.com

www.MiraclesRock.com

Instagram = 1) ajtalkaboutsex & 2) johncampbell9988

Twitter = 1) @AJTalkAboutSex & 2) @MiraclesRock

Books:

Brain Sex – Dr Anne Moir and David Jessel

A Mind to Crime – Dr Anne Moir and David Jessel

Why Men Don't Iron – Dr Anne & Bill Moir

CURRENTLY IN DEVELOPMENT: Dr Annie & John Campbell of East Sussex in the UK are working with Fearless Literary to develop *SoulSex at 70 (or Any Other Age)* that will summarise their work as spiritual sex educators.

Anna Grace Taylor

Anna Grace Taylor is an Angel Therapist, Spiritual Mentor, Healer, Author, Singer and Speaker, who has been featured on BBC Radio and Hay House Radio.

Using her natural intuitive gifts, developed by years of training and experience, Anna connects with Divine love and guidance to support people with all aspects of life and often acts as a catalyst for transformation for people all over the world.

Born eleven weeks prematurely and with Cerebral Palsy, Anna took her first independent steps at the age of six and learned to walk twice more, following major surgery and long-term illness in her teens.

I first met Anna in 2016 at the Love Seminar that I held in Arundel, West Sussex. She is such a bright and gentle soul who has inspired me immensely. She is bold and courageous as well as fun and feminine. Her work and music is heaven sent, and I love her authentic and shining light, which always beams wherever she goes.

What is your understanding of a Spiritual Awakening?

Now I would say it is about remembering who you really are: that you are a Divine being having a spiritual experience. But back when it all started I didn't understand what was really happening. I was very young and had been unwell, and at the age of 14 I needed leg surgery as I was told it would help me with my walking. I hoped that it would give me more freedom; but unfortunately, after the operations, I became very unwell, and life as I knew it fell apart.

I was always very sensitive to energy as a child and remember hearing 'something' call my name, but I had no concept of what this could be. In my teenage years the sensitivity became more heightened and I remember going into a restaurant and feeling really sick and couldn't understand why. Later I came to understand that I was picking up on the energy of the people in the room and it felt extremely overwhelming for me.

I started to ask questions about why this was happening, and at the age of 15 I was very fortunate to discover aromatherapy, reflexology and healing. The different therapists I met were very supportive to me at that time, and whilst experiencing healing I naturally started to feel energy and now had someone to ask what I was feeling. Up to that point I had no other access to this kind of information and I just thought it was me and that I was weird and sensitive. These people helped me realise that I wasn't 'wrong' and they would reassure me immensely.

My parents didn't understand what was happening regarding these strange experiences, understandably so, as they were not aware of spirit and such things, so it was a relief that I was now being heard and understood.

All the dreams I had of living a 'normal' life seemed impossible due to my physical disability and illness, and I felt different to everyone and misunderstood. I didn't have a lot of fun like other teenagers, but I found hope in my older spiritual friends. I would see flashes of light out of the corner of my eye, and by the time I was 18 I started to understand what all these feelings and experiences were.

At 21 I had a very profound experience. I saw a huge light in my room. It was the most loving and peaceful thing I have ever experienced and I knew it was an Angel. I soon found myself wanting to know more and I went on an Angel Therapy Course in Ireland. This took me to another level of understanding, and it was such a relief to meet a group of people who saw the world just like me and I no longer felt alone. I learned things in that week that helped empower me, and I knew I had found the reason for my pain and the reason for being me. I released a lot, and although that resulted in me feeling quite nauseous, it was equally comforting to know I was clearing old energy and pain from my past.

That course was such a big wake-up call, and within weeks my life started to change. I had found my power and it was a massive shift, and I could now see myself through different eyes. I had gained some tools to support me and I embraced my sensitivity as a superpower not a burden.

A year later I went to America and I started to share angel readings with people, and I felt like I had found a sense of purpose. I also realised I could share my voice with people through my singing. I was doing things that I loved, and it was so freeing and a big part of my awakening. I was very determined to follow my own path and be true to myself, and I always follow my heart and come back to love.

I have seen that things can be over spiritualised with a lot of hierarchy and comparison, which instead of joining can actually separate. We are all spiritual beings, and so to do something to make you feel that you are a spiritual person can actually have the opposite effect.

I want to help people and make things better for them and heal them, but I am aware that I am not the healer and that any healing that takes places comes through me and is not of me. We can make a difference, but by being who we are and showing people that they can remember who they are too.

A quote that has always helped me, which I discovered at a healing centre, was a big part of my awakening: "I would not interfere with any creed of yours or want to appear that I have all the cures, there is so much to know, so many things are true, the way my feet must go may not be right for you and so I give this spark of what is light for me, to guide you through the dark, but not to tell you what to do." Anon

To me that is what we are here for; we are guiding lights and way-showers in some form, but we can't make it better for each other or fix anyone. My awakening was to remember that we are always enough, even if our mind and bodies might try to tell us differently.

My practice is quite simple and I can come back to my centre a lot quicker now. I know I am always loved and supported and I am going to be okay. Being authentic and real is so important and 'the work' is to include all parts of ourselves. I have learnt to honour my feelings and my body will always let me know – I feel I know who I am now.

What is the one little nugget or gift you would offer someone who is going through the awakening journey or who is just starting to see things differently?

There is a part of you, your Divine self who knows exactly what you are doing and your life is made for you and not against you. It is not punishing you, and even if you feel really challenged or different, know that there is so much more to your life than you know right now. We can forget that there is so much possibility – life always changes. Wherever you are in this moment feel it fully – get mad, get sad, ask for help so you can move through your feelings; and as you do, you'll begin to feel even more connected to yourself and your life. Stay present without trying to work it out or make yourself wrong. Keep it simple and you won't get so overwhelmed by the future. You are enough now and you don't have to know all the answers. You never will. You don't have to be perfect as a human being because as a Divine being you already are.

Contact Details:
www.annagracetaylor.com

Book: *Messages of Grace: 111 Notes of Love and Guidance*

Gabrielle Anya Rafello

Gabrielle is an energy healer, teacher, mentor and creative, who has been supporting the energy of people and spaces for many years. I can't really remember when I first met her. We were both on the Sussex 'spiritual scene' and our paths crossed on various occasions at different events. Gabrielle has such a genuine, gentle and clear energy, and is one of those beautiful souls who seems to work quietly in the background and needs no obvious status, yet makes a huge difference through all that she does and by being who she is. She created and runs a beautiful centre in West Sussex called The Koorana Centre, which inspires creativity, spirituality and well-being, and is the way Gabrielle supports her local and extended community.

What is your understanding of a Spiritual Awakening?

It's becoming aware of a greater understanding of who we really are and knowing that we have a connection to a creative energy Source, and through that Source, we are completely united and linked together.

It was a gradual awakening for me. I had always been sensitive as a child, and I always thought there was far more to life than just what I saw. At the age of 10, I had an out of body experience, whilst running a relay race with three other girls on my school sports day. The girl before me dropped the baton and I had to pick it up and endeavour to make up the extra time. As I was running, I had such a strong feeling that I was out of my body, looking down on myself running, and somehow, we managed to win the race! I had another experience when I was a teenager and had been attending church with my mother; afterwards I felt such a supreme feeling of joy, bliss with a complete sense of oneness with spirit.

I could be quite anxious and fearful as a child, and for me

creativity was key. I would lose myself in anything that was using my hands, making things, art, etc. I would also be the child who would stare out of the window and be in my own world of imagination and dreams. I was always very curious and looking for answers. I went to art school and being different there was a good thing. Unfortunately, there were a lot of things going on inside of me and some of the abandonment issues that happened as a child were beginning to surface. I didn't realise back then, that my thoughts were creating my reality and I was attracting relationships and situations that were mirroring my childhood insecurities. I just numbed out and shut down, which I came to understand was very normal when one feels so overwhelmed with life.

I eventually got married and had two beautiful sons, and when my youngest was born, and I held him in my arms for the first time, I felt an amazing feeling of recognition and unconditional love, the likes of which I had never felt for anyone before – it was incredible. Seeing him just made me realise that we had been together before, and from that point on my awakening really started to happen.

I started to become interested in metaphysical topics and even though I had always been interested in self-help from an early age, buying *Think and Grow Rich* by Napoleon Hill at just 14 years of age, I was ready to expand my mind even more. I had one particular Angel book, which when I picked it up, would result in such an amazing feeling, as well as sensing someone standing next to me.

As I continued to open up, I learnt about reiki and energy healing, which at that time was such a powerful tool for me. However, there were still times of feeling depressed and going into the darkness, and when my husband and I were going through our divorce, a lot of fear and inner turmoil came to the surface. I realised I had to learn to surrender it and I was also wanting to break free from the material world, which just seemed so false to me and I knew it couldn't bring me the peace I was seeking. Everyone talked about surrender, but no one really told you how to do it – I discovered that this was the secret and that the Universe can only really step in once you have asked for help, and then will guide you to the solution you are seeking.

The clearing process could seem chaotic at times, knocking me off my centre, but I always felt better once the old energy had moved through me. I liken it to a storm brewing: you can feel the tension and static in the air, and as soon as the storm passes, the air is clearer and you can breathe again.

I now find that I'm in a constant state of connection, and quite often my answers to questions come in just as I am waking up in the morning, when I am relaxed and still half asleep.

I can feel Divinity, and I know it's within me and within everything in the cosmos. It is the energy behind everything that is alive and living and well. It gives me a sense of upliftment, confidence, flow, trust and something I can always fall back into which will always catch me. I also feel it when I'm with animals and in nature, which gives me a sense of greater ease within. We don't need to strive for it, but just relax into it.

There is so much evidence of this energy, and the more we believe in it, the more it will grow. You may feel it whilst gardening, singing a song, writing, performing a piece of music. All these things elevate our energy and put us in touch with this life Source. It's not a luxury to put ourselves first, it is a necessity. Once we love ourselves wholly, then we can love another wholly. If we ignore our own needs, we are not serving our children either, because they learn from us and mirror our behaviour.

What top tip would you give to someone who is awakening?

I would recommend keeping a diary or journal. I have found this very helpful as it gets things out of my head and on to paper. This in turn helps my higher power to flow through me. Getting out in nature is also so important, as well as listening to music and being with like-minded people.

We are living in an amazing time with so many resources, amazing books and teachers. Reach out, take action and choose what is right for you. Take one step, even if it's a very small step...

Gabrielle can be found at:

www.gabrielleanyarafello.com and www.thekooranacentre.com

Kat Byles

Kat Byles is a Business and Creativity Consultant with 25 years' experience working with pioneers, entrepreneurs and global brands making a difference, including Homeless World Cup, Nike, UEFA, Vodafone Foundation, Good Energy, Beyond Sport, Eric Cantona, Desmond Tutu, Colin Farrell and Lewis Hamilton.

Whilst building a business with purpose made a difference, Kat experienced burnout at just 42. Her intuition led her to Antigua and Barbuda in the Caribbean, to walk barefoot on the sand, float in the turquoise sea, watch the sunset on the horizon and eat mangos from the tree. She credits this immersion in nature with restoring her wellness and creativity. Inspiration for the True Business model then flowed. While traditional business leads with profit, True Business leads with your heart in alignment with Source. Kat is currently writing the book *True Business: unleash your heart's wisdom on what you were born for*. She lives in Antigua, where she runs the True Business School online.

I met Kat in March 2017, just five months after my mother passed away. I was guided to go on her Antigua Retreat, not only to open my mind to what my business and purpose were, but to be in a beautiful healing environment. Antigua stole my heart and soothed my soul, and I found my freedom and childlike innocence by swimming in the beautiful turquoise seas. I was incredibly inspired by Kat's journey and her teaching around creating a heart-centred business, and her passion is tangible, whilst her knowledge for creating a meaningful way of living and working is second to none.

What does awakening mean to you?

It's a deeper awareness of myself and the energy of life, which creates a different experience of the world.

In my early teens, there was no one around who understood

the awakening process. In my early 20s this led to drugs and an eating disorder – I was completely out of alignment with my true nature. I did, however, always know that within me there was a strength and deep power that had my back. I knew I'd be okay.

I've always had awareness about the awe of life, particularly in nature, a connection to an energy greater than myself. A strong empathy and intuition gave me information and insights into others, which felt overwhelming, and at such a young age, I didn't know what to do with those feelings. When I shared this with others they didn't really understand me. I was "overly sensitive". I struggled at school, which I hated. Some saw me as having a rebellious streak; however, this was not the case, I just didn't fit 'the norm'. Thankfully I can now embrace and love this part of myself. It is what makes me creative and pioneering. It's a gift.

At the beginning of the grand awakening, nothing was working – my job, boyfriend, friendships. This was an uncomfortable precursor to the full-on earthquake that shook me awake. Then it felt like a choice of life or death.

I was working in an office in Slough – like Ricky Gervais' TV series *The Office* – which was a big contrast to a creative year living in Barcelona the year before. The office environment literally made me sick. I was throwing up 14 times per day. I lost a lot of weight, felt anxious and had severe panic attacks. The breaking point was a panic attack at work. I ran home and my mum took me straight to the doctor, who prescribed Valium and also referred me to a psychiatric hospital, where I was prescribed Prozac. I wanted to stop taking drugs, not take more! I knew I had to go within and do it my own way. I said no to medication. My body is very sensitive and carries a lot of wisdom. This was a very loud signal that I was in the wrong place at work and in my life.

My parents didn't know how to deal with what was happening, but they found me a counsellor who was brilliant.

As I started counselling, I had no idea what my feelings were or why I was so angry. I went for three years, but it was two life-changing sessions working with my imagination and inner world that changed the course of my life.

It was a family awakening too. My mum went on to help parents with children with eating disorders for 15 years. We all learned to listen to each other and speak with honesty and understanding. There was a lot of blame, shame and all kinds of crazy stuff to work through, but as a result we came to love, like and respect each other so much more. Now I watch my 8-year-old niece already articulating her emotions, needs and boundaries clearly, and I'm in awe.

What books or teachers were helpful to you during your awakening?

The Celestine Prophecy by James Redfield was the first time that someone articulated what I was experiencing in a way that I felt someone understood.

The Artist's Way by Julia Cameron helped me recover my creativity and writing; the Morning Pages became a tool helping me to realise I was a writer and could write things into being.

Twenty years later, *The Surrender Experiment* by Michael Singer helped me to let go of my egoic mind and surrender to the flow of life.

More recently Simon Haas's *Yoga and the Dark Night of the Soul*. I worked with Simon on the first edit and each chapter arrived at just the right time. It's a classic.

What have you come to know about yourself?

That my heart is my inner compass. The wisdom is within me, and when I listen, life is far, far better. When I create my life in alignment with my inner being and go with the flow, everything is peaceful and harmonious. I'm more creative and vital. I know this wisdom and guidance is always there even in challenging and dark moments.

That I love being in Antigua and need to live by the ocean. This is my source of divine connection; it connects me to the life force of our planet. Some people go to church, but for me, it's an early morning or sunset swim that sustains me. My body and heart hurt when I see nature destroyed. I need connection, community and creativity to thrive with deep, real relationships.

I believe that to support our own well-being, creativity has to be at the heart of our business. I love working with others to help them tune into their heart's inner compass, which in turn supports them to discover their true nature and purpose. It's a joy for me to see clients open up like this and learn to trust their own way in business, which is so very different to the old business model, where we are managed and not given the opportunity to express our true self.

What else would you like to share with those who are awakening?

Trust the awakening is a gift, leading you to deeper love, peace, authenticity, and integrity, and is a far more fulfilling place to be. Know that when you surrender you receive support.

It doesn't have to be traumatic. Learn to listen to your inner guidance and discover what you need. Then learn to stop denying yourself what you need. It takes courage to listen and follow your heart's wisdom, your soul calling, but it's so worth it. It is your life's work and the greatest adventure.

Contact Details:
Email: kat@katbyles.com
Website: https://www.true-business-school.com
Instagram: @truebusinessschool

Further Support and Inspiration

I would like to offer to you an index of books and teachers, which I have personally found inspiring, helpful, insightful and incredibly beneficial along the path. Please don't feel you have to explore any of these pathways, but know that they are there if you feel so drawn.

I wish to remind you that our paths are unique, and what resonates with one, may not resonate with another. You may be right at the beginning of your SA and have no idea where to turn, you may be further down the line and wanting to deepen your connection or you may be at a transitional point and unsure in what direction to go. Either way, trust your heart to guide you and pray for help in choosing what is going to support you on the next stage of your awakening. Enjoy!

A Course in Miracles (ACIM) Foundation for Inner Peace (A spiritual book standing on its own)

ACIM Related Teachers
David Hoffmeister
Ken Wapnick
Robert Holden
Alan Cohen
Gary Renard
Cindy Lora-Renard
Marianne Williamson
Kirsten Buxton
Nouk Sanchez

Metaphysics & General Spirituality
Eckhart Tolle
Louise L. Hay

Dr Wayne Dyer
Pam Grout

Quantum Physics & Law of Attraction
Jerry & Esther Hicks
Florence Scovel-Shinn
Dr Joe Dispenza
David R. Hamilton

And the Rest...
Byron Katie – *Loving What Is; A Thousand Names for Joy; A Mind at Home with Itself; I Need Your Love – Is That True?*
Jeff Foster – *Falling in Love with Where You Are; The Deepest Acceptance*
Eileen Caddy – *Footprints on the Path; Opening Doors Within*
Michael A. Singer – *The Untethered Soul; The Surrender Experiment*
Daniel Ladinsky – *Love Poems from God*
Julia Cameron – *The Artist's Way*
John Randolph Price – *The Abundance Book*
Kahlil Gibran – *The Prophet*
Susan Jeffers – *Feel the Fear and Do It Anyway*
Thich Nhat Hanh – *The Energy of Prayer*

Music To Inspire
Deva Premal & Miten
Lucinda Drayton & Bliss
Jason Mraz
Neda Boin
Sam Garrett
Ajeet Kaur
Snatam Kaur
Ashana
India Arie
Lex van Someren
Peter Kater

Acknowledgments

First and foremost, I wish to say thank you to Sarah Cox, who was the first person to inform me that I was going through a SA. I am eternally grateful for your love, your light, your encouragement and your truth. I know we were destined to meet, and somewhere in the quantum field our hearts knew what needed to be done in this lifetime. I'll meet you in that place again, dear friend, and bless you and love you always.

My Children – The gift you have given me, Daniel and Emma, has been and continues to be my greatest learning. I am beyond thankful for our journey together in this lifetime, and know without doubt that our soul agreement has helped me to wake up. I wish you eternal peace, joy, happiness and boundless love. Fly free and shine your light and know I am but a heartbeat away, wherever my physical form may be. I am so blessed to have you in my life.

My Family – Dear Mum and Dad, wow what a journey – thank you for everything. I am honoured to have been your daughter and will see you soon on the other side – can't wait to see you again beyond the body and in the light.

Steve and Neil – brothers in arms and a journey beyond time. I love you.

My Mighty Companions – Alex Scott, Celia Stuart, Mary Adams, Helen Thatcher, John Campbell – thank you for shining the light and illuminating the way. I love you.

Friends, clients and lovers – Deep gratitude for mirroring back to me everything I needed to learn. You were all my teachers, and I honour you and thank you for being in my life.

Chris Marchant – Our destiny was written before we came down and I thank you for everything we shared together. I am so grateful and I know our love is eternal.

Laura Ball – Thank you for helping me with this book and

being an immense support in many ways. Your unwavering patience and laughter has been a blessing. We were brought together for this purpose by divine intervention but also to nourish a friendship beyond the written word.

The teachers and way-showers – No names here, as there were so many, but all I can say is from my heart to yours, I THANK YOU – I LOVE YOU!

Endnotes

All quotes from *A Course in Miracles*, copyright ©1992, 1999, 2007 by the Foundation for Inner Peace, 448 Ignacio Blvd. #306, Novato, CA 94949, www.acim.org and info@acim.org, used with permission.

Here is how to reference the quotes used in A Course In Miracles (ACIM)

- T = Text
- W = Workbook
- M = Manual for Teachers
- Chapter
- Section
- Paragraph
- Line

1. *The Game of Life and How to Play It*. Florence Scovel-Shinn
2. ACIM, W-187.3:2
3. Sarah Cox – taken from her interview transcript
4. Gabrielle Anya Rafello – taken from her interview transcript
5. ACIM, T-21.In.1:7
6. With permission from Elizabeth Gordon – www.facebook.com/encompassyourlife
7. Annie Campbell – taken from her interview transcript
8. With permission under 'fair use' from the Rumi Network
9. With kind permission from Hay House
10. ACIM, W-154.7
11. With permission from Cecil Corsiatto
12. Sarah Cox – taken from her interview transcript
13. Kat Byles – taken from her interview transcript
14. John Campbell – taken from his interview transcript

15. ACIM, L-153

16. With kind permission from Robert Holden – taken from his book *Be Happy*

17. ACIM, T-V.18:2-6

18. With kind permission from Hay House. Taken from *Meditations to Heal Your Life* by Louise L. Hay.

19. John Campbell – taken from his interview transcript

20. Sarah Cox – taken from her interview transcript

21. ACIM, T-17-IV.3:3

22. With kind permission from Nicole Lyons – Canadian author and poet

23. Taken from Byron Katie's free information booklet which she offers for everyone wishing to practice The Work. For full details and to download the worksheets go to her website: www.thework.com

24. All of the wording from the Prophet is under public domain and therefore no copyright or approval needed – as per the Gibran National Committee

25. ACIM, L-140.10:1-4

26. ACIM, W-part II.8:1-2

27. Rumi – with permission under 'fair use' as per the Rumi Network

28. ACIM, W-26-IX.6:1

29. ACIM, L-169

30. Anna Grace Taylor – taken from her interview transcript

31. ACIM, L-84-3:2

32. ACIM, M-1-1:1-13

About the Author

Ann-Marie's passions are all things spiritual, metaphysical and quantum, but it wasn't always that way. She came from a background of believing that life was black or white, with a need to 'see it before she would believe it' mentality, but she eventually discovered that neither was true.

After a series of tragic events and an experience she calls 'The Falling', she was metaphorically and literally brought to her knees. Her life then took on a completely different trajectory, resulting in a slow but profound dismantling of her identity.

She had inadvertently found herself on a Spiritual Awakening path, which guided her to explore the world of alternative and holistic health, leading her to train as a Holistic Therapist, Hypnotherapist, NLP Practitioner and Meditation Facilitator.

She came to realise that there was, in fact, a much bigger plan at play and that there was a divine presence leading her life. With the mantra of 'show me the truth' as her daily prayer, Ann-Marie's biggest change was still to come as she found herself on the threshold of training to be a multifaith minister. From a person who could barely say the word 'God' without a visceral reaction of distaste, this was a pretty big turnaround.

Ann-Marie has embraced the simplicity of a guided spiritual life and now trusts in a loving presence, which she knows is available to everyone. Her heart's desire is to help those who are ready and willing to 'wake up' too. This has resulted in the creation of her first book, which was initiated by 'another voice' prompting her to write it.

Ann-Marie lives in the UK and facilitates spiritual workshops, retreats, meditation groups, as well as offering one-to-one mentoring for those who find themselves awakening too.

www.ann-mariemarchant.co.uk
www.facebook.com/Annmariemarchantminister

O-BOOKS

SPIRITUALITY

O is a symbol of the world, of oneness and unity; this eye
represents knowledge and insight. We publish titles on general
spirituality and living a spiritual life. We aim to inform and help
you on your own journey in this life.
If you have enjoyed this book, why not tell other readers by
posting a review on your preferred book site?

Recent bestsellers from O-Books are:

Heart of Tantric Sex
Diana Richardson
Revealing Eastern secrets of deep love and intimacy to Western
couples.
Paperback: 978-1-90381-637-0 ebook: 978-1-84694-637-0

Crystal Prescriptions
The A-Z guide to over 1,200 symptoms and their healing crystals
Judy Hall
The first in the popular series of eight books, this handy little
guide is packed as tight as a pill-bottle with crystal remedies for
ailments.
Paperback: 978-1-90504-740-6 ebook: 978-1-84694-629-5

Take Me To Truth
Undoing the Ego
Nouk Sanchez, Tomas Vieira
The best-selling step-by-step book on shedding the Ego, using the
teachings of *A Course In Miracles*.
Paperback: 978-1-84694-050-7 ebook: 978-1-84694-654-7

The 7 Myths about Love...Actually!
The Journey from your HEAD to the HEART of your SOUL
Mike George
Smashes all the myths about LOVE.
Paperback: 978-1-84694-288-4 ebook: 978-1-84694-682-0

The Holy Spirit's Interpretation of the New Testament
A Course in Understanding and Acceptance
Regina Dawn Akers
Following on from the strength of *A Course In Miracles*, NTI
teaches us how to experience the love and oneness of God.
Paperback: 978-1-84694-085-9 ebook: 978-1-78099-083-5

The Message of A Course In Miracles
A translation of the Text in plain language
Elizabeth A. Cronkhite
A translation of *A Course in Miracles* into plain, everyday
language for anyone seeking inner peace. The companion
volume, *Practicing A Course In Miracles*, offers practical lessons
and mentoring.
Paperback: 978-1-84694-319-5 ebook: 978-1-84694-642-4

Your Simple Path
Find Happiness in every step
Ian Tucker
A guide to helping us reconnect with what is really important in our lives.
Paperback: 978-1-78279-349-6 ebook: 978-1-78279-348-9

365 Days of Wisdom
Daily Messages To Inspire You Through The Year
Dadi Janki
Daily messages which cool the mind, warm the heart and guide you along your journey.
Paperback: 978-1-84694-863-3 ebook: 978-1-84694-864-0

Body of Wisdom
Women's Spiritual Power and How it Serves
Hilary Hart
Bringing together the dreams and experiences of women across the world with today's most visionary spiritual teachers.
Paperback: 978-1-78099-696-7 ebook: 978-1-78099-695-0

Dying to Be Free
From Enforced Secrecy to Near Death to True Transformation
Hannah Robinson
After an unexpected accident and near-death experience, Hannah Robinson found herself radically transforming her life, while a remarkable new insight altered her relationship with her father, a practising Catholic priest.
Paperback: 978-1-78535-254-6 ebook: 978-1-78535-255-3

Quantum Bliss
The Quantum Mechanics of Happiness, Abundance, and Health
George S. Mentz
Quantum Bliss is the breakthrough summary of success and spirituality secrets that customers have been waiting for.
Paperback: 978-1-78535-203-4 ebook: 978-1-78535-204-1

The Upside Down Mountain
Mags MacKean
A must-read for anyone weary of chasing success and happiness – one woman's inspirational journey swapping the uphill slog for the downhill slope.
Paperback: 978-1-78535-171-6 ebook: 978-1-78535-172-3

Your Personal Tuning Fork
The Endocrine System
Deborah Bates
Discover your body's health secret, the endocrine system, and 'twang' your way to sustainable health!
Paperback: 978-1-84694-503-8 ebook: 978-1-78099-697-4

Readers of ebooks can buy or view any of these bestsellers by clicking on the live link in the title. Most titles are published in paperback and as an ebook. Paperbacks are available in traditional bookshops. Both print and ebook formats are available online.
Find more titles and sign up to our readers' newsletter at http://www.johnhuntpublishing.com/mind-body-spirit
Follow us on Facebook at https://www.facebook.com/OBooks/
and Twitter at https://twitter.com/obooks